DATE DUE

MᴬDᴏɴɴA

BOOKS BY THE AUTHOR

Madonna
Everybody Loves Oprah!
Donahue: The Man Women Love
Dan Rather
Here's Erma: The Bombecking of America
The Prince and the Princess
Two Royal Women
Ivana
The Money Messiahs
The Money Market Book
The First Five Minutes
The Last Five Minutes
All in the First Family (with Bill Adler)

M^aDonna

THE BOOK

Norman King

WILLIAM MORROW AND COMPANY, INC.
NEW YORK

It is the policy of William Morrow and Company, Inc., and its imprints and affiliates, recognizing the importance of preserving what has been written, to print the books we publish on acid-free paper, and we exert our best efforts to that end.

Library of Congress Cataloging-in-Publication Data

King, Norman.
    Madonna : the book / by Norman King.
    p.   cm.
    ISBN 0–688–10389–8
    1. Madonna, 1959–   . 2. Rock Musicians—United States—Biography. 3. Motion picture actors and actresses—United States—Biography. I. Title.
ML420.M1387K5 1992
782.42166'092—dc20
    [B]   91–22621 CIP MN

Printed in the United States of America

First Edition

1 2 3 4 5 6 7 8 9 10

BOOK DESIGN BY LISA STOKES

To the second love of my life, the one and only Friars Club, and, to my friends Buddy Hackett and Henny Youngman.

It's true. There's no business like show business and no people like show people.

CONTENTS

1

MOTOWN

It was a very special moment in history. The 1950s, with just the beginning of rock and roll dimly foreshadowed in the laid-back, father-image style of the Eisenhower years, was about to give way to the permissive, high-flying, anything-goes 1960s—but the change had not yet occurred.

For the most part America was prosperous, buttoned-down, and suburbia-oriented. But there were signs in the offing, signs that things would never be the same again, not only in America, but all over the rest of the world as well.

Motown—a portmanteau word formed by combining *motor* and *town* (read: Detroit)—was the world distribution point of fast cars, and big gas guzzlers were the symbols of the power of America everywhere. It was also the center of another and more specific "Motown"—an up-and-coming record company that would make its mark on the world of rock and roll in the very near future. It was the generating point of Berry Gordy's Motown Records.

As if fast cars and rock and roll were not enough to mark Motown as an important center of the new universe of the 1960s, on August 16, 1959, some hundred miles north of Motown in Bay City, Michigan, Madonna Louise Veronica Ciccone (pronounced in Florentine Italian "Chi-cone-ay") was born to Silvio and Madonna Ciccone.

Named for her mother, a somewhat unusual thing in a Catholic family, Madonna Ciccone was born at her grandmother's house in Bay City, where the family was living at the time. Shortly afterward the Ciccones would move to Pontiac, Michigan, one of the many suburbs in and around Motown, U.S.A. Bay City was Madonna's mother's hometown.

Madonna was the first girl born to the Ciccones, who already had five boys. Silvio, her father, was a first-generation American, whose father and mother had come over to America from Italy to settle in a town just outside Pittsburgh, Pennsylvania. Silvio's father decided at an early age that Pittsburgh had plenty of work for an able-bodied male, which he considered himself to be, so he dedicated his life to serving in the steel mills.

The newly arrived Ciccones lived there in what Madonna later described as a "sort of an Italian ghetto-type neighborhood." In addition, Madonna's grandmother and grandfather spoke no English at all. A working-class couple, they had no formal education. They had six children, all boys; Silvio was the youngest, the smartest, and the most determined of them all. Determined to shake the grime and coal dust of Pittsburgh from his person at the first possible moment.

Silvio took enough abuse as a child from his peers about his humble beginnings, and it did not take this stubborn young man long to promise himself to rise above the just-over-poverty level in which he spent his early years. Silvio was the first Ciccone to get a college education, and in college he trained himself for a career in engineering. One fine day after he had earned his degree in engineering, Silvio moved to Michigan, selecting the automobile industry as the place where he would settle down to move onward and upward in what was then a prosperous, expanding America.

He joined the air force and was in uniform when he met the woman he was going to marry—Madonna Fortin. She was a French Canadian, born in Bay City, Michigan, just across the lake from Canada, and the sister of one of Silvio's best friends. They were soon married, and Madonna and Silvio settled down in Bay City temporarily with Madonna Fortin's sister.

After moving to Pontiac several years later, they would eventually settle in Rochester, a smaller town about five miles north of Pontiac. Rochester is now known as Rochester Hills, making the place sound a great deal more dignified and up-and-coming than simply Rochester.

"She was very beautiful," Madonna once described her mother. "I look like her. I have my father's eyes, but I have my mother's smile and a lot of her facial structure." At no time could it ever be said that Madonna was modest about her looks, or, for that matter, about any part of her persona, including her brains.

She was brought up in a traditionally strict Catholic home. It seems obvious now that the rebel Madonna was always within the seemingly compliant, obedient Madonna at this early date, and that the rebel was just waiting to break loose and take over the entire personality at the appropriate hour.

"My father was very strict and a disciplinarian—we had to go to church every morning before we went to school. When we got home, we'd get changed, do our chores, do our home-work, and eat supper. I wasn't even allowed to watch tele-vision until late in my teens. My father didn't like us having idle time on our hands."

He kept them busy, and if he ran out of assignments for the children, their mother could always supply a half dozen more chores to perform.

"If we didn't have homework, he'd find us something to do around the house. He was very adamant about us being productive," she said. Not only did her mother and father stress Catholicism to her, but her grandmother did as well. "When I was tiny, my grandmother used to beg me not to go with boys, to love Jesus, and to be a good girl. I grew up with two images of women: the Virgin and the Whore."

This ambivalence is of course not unusual in individuals brought up in a strictly religious home such as Madonna's was. One other thing Madonna remembered about her mother. "She kept getting pregnant at the same time every year." There were five boys in the family at the time Madonna was born; eventually there would be two more girls, but not by Madonna's real mother.

One of Madonna's first memorable impressions was of watching her parents dancing the twist together to the records of Chubby Checker and Sam Cooke. By this time the Ciccones had moved to Pontiac and were living in an integrated neighborhood.

"We were one of the only white families," Madonna recalled, "and all the kids had Motown and black [record] stuff. And they had yard dances in their backyard, little forty-five turntables and a stack of records, and everyone just danced in the driveway and the backyard."

In spite of occasional relaxation and recreation, Madonna's life was rigidly structured. "My father was very strong. I don't agree with some of his values [now], but he did have integrity, and if he told us not to do something, *he* didn't do it either. A lot of parents tell their kids not to smoke cigarettes—but *they* smoke cigarettes. Or they give you some idea of sexual modesty—but my father lived that way. He believed that making love to someone is a very sacred thing and it shouldn't happen until after you are married. He stuck to those beliefs, and that represented a very strong person to me. He was my role model."

Silvio Ciccone's firmness and integrity shaped her because she understood and respected his strength of will and recognized what he was trying to do with his life.

"The thing is," Madonna observed, "if my father hadn't been strict, I wouldn't be who I am today. I think that his strictness taught me a certain amount of discipline that has helped me in my life and my career and also made me work harder for things, whether for acceptance or the privilege to do things."

Early on, Madonna learned the tricks that were to come in handy later. "From when I was very young," she said, "I just knew that being a girl and being charming in a feminine sort of way could get me a lot of things, and I milked it for everything I could."

She admitted later, "I was my father's favorite. I knew how to wrap him around my finger. I knew there was another way to go besides saying, 'No, I'm not going to do it,' and I employed those techniques."

Madonna had been born with enough ambition to fuel a half dozen hard-driving people. She had grown up watching her mother and father dancing to Motown sounds, and she herself wanted to dance too. She was never modest about it, never humble.

"At family reunions," she recounted, "I'd climb on a table and start dancing. If I didn't get people's attention that way, I'd make some noise."

Madonna was not quite five when she sensed that something was very wrong in her family. That is, her mother seemed to grow remote and depressed. In fact her mother was ill; the breast cancer from which she suffered had been misdiagnosed. She was slowly, inexorably dying. Typically she kept her feelings to herself, her fear locked up inside her, and never let on to her children. She never complained.

"I remember she was really sick and was sitting on the couch," Madonna recalled. "I went up to her and I remember climbing on her back."

Madonna clamored, "Play with me, play with me!" but her mother failed to respond.

"She couldn't," Madonna said. "And she started crying and I got really angry with her and I remember, like, pounding her back with my fist."

"Why are you doing this?" Madonna cried.

"Then I realized she was crying," Madonna recalled. And after a moment she guessed at the truth. "I remember feeling stronger than she was. I was so little and put my arms around her, and I could feel her body underneath me sobbing, and I felt like she was the child. I stopped tormenting her after that. That was the turning point when I knew. I think that made me grow up fast. I knew I could be either sad and weak and not in control or I could just take control and say, 'It's going to get better.'"

Finally her mother was moved to the hospital, where she spent the best part of a year. "I saw my father going through changes also. He was devastated." Madonna's father would take them all to the hospital to visit. "I remember my mother was always cracking up and making jokes. She was really funny, so it wasn't so awful to go and visit her there."

One thing stuck in Madonna's mind. "I remember that right before she died, she asked for a hamburger. She wanted to eat a hamburger because she couldn't eat anything for so long, and I thought that was very funny."

Madonna was six and a half when her mother died. This turn of events was traumatic and dislocating for her. Silvio was unable to keep the large family going by himself, since he was away at the Chrysler plant all day, so the children were bundled off to separate residences of relatives for the time being.

Then Silvio hired a housekeeper, who got the place in order once again, after which the children returned.

"If I couldn't have a mother to take care of me," Madonna reasoned, "then I was going to take care of myself." She determined that she was going to make sure she lived a very "special" life. Interestingly enough, Madonna had set the wheels in motion for her own American Dream Life.

Now that they were back with their father, the children realized that things were really not the same and would never be the same again. Madonna had become the main female of the house, and somehow she was enjoying the role. It was her lot, since she was the only woman in the family, to hold them all together. It was at this point that Madonna began to perfect those tricks of compelling attention from her father— and of manipulating him into doing whatever she wanted him to do.

Unfortunately for Madonna, her success at getting her own way alienated her from the rest of her siblings. They were annoyed that she had such pull, leaving the rest of them to do all the work and get little credit.

They began turning on her, calling her selfish and too smart and just awful. Once they even hung her up on the clothesline in the backyard by her underpants. Besides that, unexpected quirks began to appear in Madonna's personality, which was still in the very formative stages. She seemed somehow on a doomsday kick.

"I've inherited some of my father's qualities," she once said, naming "stubbornness and being a killjoy" as the main ones. It was the "killjoy" aspect of her character that seemed to surface in those young years—and it was totally unwelcome to everyone who knew her.

Madonna explained: "If I go out with friends, I'm usually the first one who wants to go home, in spite of their protests. When we went to visit relatives, my father would always want to go home instead of spending the night with them. That's my father in me."

Madonna had discovered the excitement of music and now bought two records: "Incense and Peppermints," by the Strawberry Alarm Clock, and "The Letter" by the Box Tops. That was in 1967. She played them all the time. But her brothers howled her down every time she put one of them on the turntable.

"They told me pop music was a pile of shit," Madonna later said. "They scratched my records so that I couldn't play them. It only made me love pop more."

Meanwhile the household was a wild and woolly background for battles and arguments galore. A string of housekeepers came and went—most of them unable to stand the fighting and the turmoil—until one came who reminded Madonna of her mother.

"Sort of like Natalie Wood," she recalled. "We all thought our father was going to marry her."

It was not to be.

And so, quite suddenly, like the short sharp shock in the Gilbert and Sullivan song, the blow was struck in Madonna's life. She was just nine, the established "mother" of the clan. Her father called them all together one night and announced that he was going to get married.

Not, however, to the housekeeper who reminded them of their mother.

Their new mother was, in Madonna's words, the Wicked Witch of the East.

"She was really gung-ho, very strict. It was hard to accept her as an authority figure and the new number-one female in my father's life. He wanted us to call her Mom, not by her first name." That first name, incidentally, was Joan.

Every day Madonna was beginning to feel more and more like Cinderella.

2

TEEN TIMES

Technically the "teens" begin with the thirteenth year and end up with the nineteenth year. Traditionally they are the years of adolescence, and include all the pains, frustrations, and joys of *being* an adolescent in a society that has made a significant *thing* of that period of growing up in the twentieth century.

Many women slide into their teen years long before thirteen. So it was with Madonna. The early disruption in her life—the death of her beloved mother at an early age and the remarriage of her father to someone Madonna did not care for—were traumatic enough to drive her into adolescence prematurely.

So, it was at age nine that Madonna "discovered boys," to use her phrase. She even got her first Valentine's Day card then. It came from someone she didn't particularly like. In the perverse manner of the young, the youth she *did* particularly like was paying no attention to her.

Her memory of it was that her idol was a boy in the fifth grade named Ronny Howard. "He had white-blond hair and sky-blue eyes," she said. "I wrote his name all over my sneakers and on the playground. I used to take off the top part of my uniform and chase him around."

In this exercise Madonna was obviously exerting one of the ambivalent phases of her personality—that part of her that represented "the Whore" as opposed to that of "the Virgin."

Some of her sexual rebellion surfaced at school. "We had to wear uniforms to [parochial] school," she said, "so I would put bright panty bloomers underneath and hang upside down on the monkey bars at recess." That gave the boys an eyeful of the young woman who did not know whether she was a witch or a saint.

The ambivalence in her character was not limited to sexual byplay. It was in her conception of skin color as well. "I always wished I was black. All my girlfriends were black . . . and all the music I listened to was black. I was incredibly jealous of all my black girlfriends because they could have braids in their hair that stuck up everywhere. So I would go through this incredible ordeal of putting wire in my hair and braiding it so I could make my hair stick up. I used to make cornrows and everything. But if being black is synonymous with having soul, then yes, I feel that I am [black]."

When she was ten years old, the family packed up its belongings in Pontiac and moved up the road—about five miles—to the smaller community then called Rochester. There Madonna became a member of the Camp Fire Girls. But her smoldering resentment against her stepmother and subconsciously against her father for marrying someone Madonna did not approve of continued unabated.

"As the oldest girl in my family, I feel like all my adolescence was spent taking care of babies," Madonna recalled. "I think that's when I really thought about how I wanted to get away from all that. I saw myself as the quintessential Cinderella."

The vision of the stepmother and the unfriendly siblings reinforced that feeling in her, spearheading the move she made not too many years later when she was only seventeen.

She used her increasing skill at dancing to good effect by giving dance lessons to boys. She would charge them a modest fee to learn the new dance steps.

"I remember the first guy I gave a lesson to. The song was 'Honky Tonk Woman' by the Rolling Stones and it was really sexy, really stomping and grinding."

Meanwhile she was beginning to grow up a bit faster physically. "When you're from a big family," she said, "everybody's really competitive with each other, so aside from just screaming really loud and doing things that got me attention, we would all get in various kinds of trouble to get my father's attention and then be punished accordingly."

She was bright, quick, and inventive. "I was really competitive in school with my grades and stuff, because my father used to give us rewards if we got A's on our report cards. It wasn't so much that I was interested in learning. My father gave us twenty-five cents for every A that we got, so I wanted to earn the most amount of money." Most of the time she did win out over her brothers and sisters.

It did not make her lot a happy one in the family circle. She was known as pushy, obnoxious, and impossible to get along with. Much of the time she did things not because she wanted to do them but because she knew that doing them would get everybody else's back up at her.

"I wanted to do everything everybody told me I could not do. I couldn't wear makeup. I couldn't wear nylons. I couldn't cut my hair. I couldn't go on dates. I couldn't even go to the movies with my friends."

And during these years the responsibilities were piling up on her at home. "I'd come home from school and there'd be diapers on the line and mouths to feed." She kept reflecting her anger back at her stepmother. "I never go out," she would complain to her, "and I don't have any pretty dresses."

In addition her father was still the tough taskmaster. He was an advocate of the ancient adage "Idle hands are the devil's workshop." In his wisdom he selected exactly the right kind of discipline that could have helped Madonna had she chosen not to revolt against it.

"Everyone in the family studied a musical instrument," Madonna recalled. "My father was really big on that. There was always music in our house—either records or the radio or someone singing in the bathtub. Noise. Lots of noise."

She studied piano for a full year, but then she quit. "Actually my teacher made me quit because I never went to the lessons. I used to hide in a ditch." She talked her father into letting her take dance lessons instead, not a bad alternative, as it later turned out.

Madonna went to three different Catholic schools, each of which was very strict and regimented. In a way the competition instilled in the students was excellent for her. It helped hone her ambition for the future, ambition that later was her most formidable character element.

Her first career inspiration was a surprise to her family. Instead of working toward singing or dancing or acting, she decided she would become a writer. "I wrote a lot of short stories and poems," she said. "But when I started a novel, I did about thirty pages and just stopped."

But stories and ideas for stories led to other fantasies—and that in turn led her to visit the old movie houses that held revivals of films from the golden era of Hollywood. And it was there that Madonna first saw the fragile and vulnerable beauty of the early queens of the cinema. In fact she fell in love with Marilyn Monroe, Judy Holliday, and Carole Lombard.

"They were all just incredibly funny and they were silly and sweet. I saw myself in them, my funniness and my need to boss people around and at the same time to be taken care of. My knowingness and my innocence. Both."

Once she had been star-struck, she became more serious about her interest in singing and dancing. She began to try out for parts in school productions and church choirs. She was now a freshman at Rochester Adams High School and had begun to start twirling the baton, doing gymnastics, and learning ballet steps.

"In her freshman and sophomore year she was a cheerleader at school," said Mary Conley-Belote, a friend in those days. "She got good grades and she was very good-looking, with [that] long, dark, gorgeous hair."

She did cause people to stop and stare at her. Doug Lee, who once dated Madonna's sister, recalled, "When she came to Adams in the ninth grade, she was the belle of the ball. Later on she tried awful hard to be different, dressing like a gypsy in school. She pretty much singled herself off from everybody else."

One thing that annoyed Lee was her predilection for singing all the time. "I used to tell her to quit singing in my car. I didn't like the way she wrecked the songs."

Madonna soon gave up on the cheerleading, deciding to concentrate on singing and dancing. Her decision soon began to pay off. She started to earn standing ovations for her song and dance performances. She even tried out for and won the lead roles in *My Fair Lady* and *The Sound of Music*.

At home the same old battle raged on. If she was not home by an early hour every night, there would be big trouble. However, her brothers were allowed to stay out late and go to pop concerts.

"I was left out," Madonna mourned. "Somewhere deep down inside of me was a frustrated little boy."

Wrong. Deep down inside her was an awakened feminist. And she played the role in her own modified manner. At home she was the demure dresser and speaker. But once she got to school, she would go to the ladies' room and change into the costume of her desired role. "I'd roll up my uniform skirt so that it was short. I'd put makeup on and change into nylon stockings." Her image and personality both underwent radical changes. "And I was incredibly flirtatious."

She loved to shock people. And in doing so, she gained a reputation for being a shameless vamp.

"My first boyfriend was when I was, I guess—gee—I think fourteen or fifteen. I fell in love with a boy named Russell. He was the only boy who would dance with me at school, because I was really wild at the high school dances and I danced completely insanely. All the guys were afraid to ask me to dance with them because I basically ignored them anyway.

"But Russell was a wild dancer [too] and he was a couple of years older and he was more sophisticated. . . . He was the [only] one who had the courage, really, [to ask me]. So he won my heart, because he wasn't afraid of me."

The teenage Madonna was also not averse to engaging in a bit of fisticuffs if it came to that. A high school friend, Carol Belanger, recalled that she and Madonna used to peek through the convent windows "to see the nuns without their habits. We found out then they had hair." And later on, Belanger said the pair of them drove to a nearby lake in a red Mustang that belonged to Madonna. There a group of rough leather-clad bikers began dropping firecrackers on them.

"Madonna yelled up and told them to knock it off. The next thing I knew, one of the biker girls came down and started hitting her in the mouth. We finally got away, but Madonna had a black eye and bruised cheek."

She was sixteen years old in 1975, and it was in that year that Madonna made a rather odd film debut, appearing in a super-8 movie, directed by a friend at school, in which the most amazing scene was one of Madonna letting her friends fry an egg on her stomach.

Those were the years of teenage rebellion against the status quo. Madonna recalled it this way:

"We laughed at the world together. We thought we were better than anybody else, and our main point of interest was boys. We liked the floozy look because our parents didn't like it. We got dressed to the nines. We got bras and stuffed them so our breasts were overlarge and wore really tight sweaters—we were sweater-girl floozies. We wore tons of lipstick and really badly applied makeup and huge beauty marks, and we wore our hair up."

Madonna would often escape to Bay City, Michigan, where her grandmother put up with her as she really was and not as she pretended to be back in Rochester. She made friends with others at Rochester Adams High School. One of them introduced her to ballet.

"She took me to ballet classes in Rochester, and that's where I meet a guy named Christopher Flynn, who saved me from my high school turmoil. He had his own ballet school. I really loved him."

It was in her junior year at high school that Madonna began to take ballet classes with Christopher Flynn. And in entering the world of ballet, she underwent another change of image. As her friend Mary Conley-Belote said, "In her junior and senior years, she cut off all her shoulder-length hair, pierced her ears, got into nuts and berries, and stopped shaving her armpits and legs." She was, according to Conley-Belote, "kind of far-out."

For good reason. Christopher Flynn was the first homosexual Catholic Madonna had ever met. "I didn't understand the concept of gay at that time," Madonna confessed later. "I was probably twelve or thirteen years old. All I knew was that my ballet teacher was *different* from everybody else. He was so alive. He had a certain theatricality about him. He made you proud of yourself."

Flynn put her to the test of self-discipline and constant practice. She showed him what she had. He remembered her as "one of the best students I've ever had, a very worldly sort of woman even as a child. We would go to gay bars, and she and I would go out and dance our asses off. People would clear away and let her go."

Madonna had never dared to visit the gay clubs in downtown Motown. With Flynn she felt safe there. And it opened up an aspect of life she had never allowed herself to think about. She observed and she digested what she was seeing. She herself had no need for the manic pleasures of drugs or inverted sex. But she saw the scene for what it was. And she knew she could live with it.

"I can see her now in tights and leotards at the barre with the rest of the students," Flynn recalled. "She had wonderful bone structure, a highly expressive face, and a truly wonderful dancer's figure, slender but shapely and long in the leg."

She liked drama at school. Her drama teacher, Bev Gibson, spotted the special "presence" that Madonna radiated. However, she saw little else in the "highly intelligent, very insightful" woman that would suggest she might be a star in the future.

If anything, Madonna struck her as a loner. "I don't remember Madonna ever having a steady boyfriend," she said. "When she went to a dance—she *loved* to dance—she was usually with a group of people. Sometimes she even danced alone, because she was such a good dancer, most of the other kids really couldn't keep up."

Madonna took ballet classes in Pontiac. Cindy Mason, a neighbor, sometimes took her there and back.

"I would drive her if Joan was busy," she recalled, naming Madonna's stepmother. "Dancing was the one thing that really made [Madonna] stand out. She didn't do much baby-sitting. She just wasn't the baby-sitting type."

Tim Lentz was technical director for the school's drama classes. He remembers Madonna. "She was real hip and very bohemian," he recalled.

In the long run it was Flynn who impressed Madonna the most. Nevertheless she confessed that her ballet lessons with him were strange encounters. "I didn't know what I was doing, really. I was with these really professional ballet dancers. I had only studied jazz up to then, so I had to work twice as hard as anybody else, and Christopher Flynn was impressed with me. He saw my body changing and how hard I worked."

She recalled the time she had her head all wrapped up in a towel, like a turban. Flynn came over to her and looked her in the eyes and said, "You know, you're really beautiful."

Madonna frowned and said, "What?" as if she had not heard him.

He said, "You have an ancient-looking face. A face like an ancient Roman statue."

Madonna was flabbergasted. "I knew that I was interesting," she said later, "and of course I was voluptuous for my age, but I'd never had a sense of myself being beautiful until he told me. The way he said it, it was an internal thing, something much deeper than superficial beauty."

Her experience with Flynn was not the usual kind of male-female attraction. "I really loved him," she said. "He was my first taste of what I thought was an artistic person."

He taught her a great deal. "He educated me," she said. "He took me to museums and told me about art. He was my mentor, my father, my imaginative lover, my brother, everything, because he understood me. He encouraged me to go to New York. He was the one who said I could do it if I wanted to."

Of all her own real brothers, Christopher Ciccone was closest to Madonna. "He was so beautiful," she recalled later, "and had girls all over him, more than any of my other brothers." What she did not know at the time was that Christopher Ciccone would become gay when he matured. "I knew *something* was different," Madonna explained thoughtfully, "but it was not clear to me exactly what."

It was a simple enough thing for Madonna to shrug it off by realizing that even though there were plenty of girls around him, and he never seemed to have a steady girlfriend, perhaps he hadn't really found the right one yet.

She remembered: "He was like a girl magnet. They all seemed incredibly fond of him and close to him in a way I hadn't seen men with women."

Soon enough she discovered the truth. After she had met with Christopher Flynn and begun dancing for him, she heard that her brother Christopher wanted to start studying ballet too.

"I brought my brother to my ballet class," she recalled, and introduced the two Christophers to one another. "I just saw something between them. I can't even tell you exactly what. But then I thought: Oh, I get it. Oh, okay! He likes men too! It was this incredible revelation, but I didn't say anything to my brother [then]. I'm not even sure *he* knew. He's two years younger than me. He was still a baby. [But] I could just *feel* something."

At the time, however, Madonna did not give voice to her thoughts, nor did her brother Christopher. It was as if the subject of homosexuality was forbidden for discussion in the Ciccone home—as, of course, it was.

The story of Christopher Flynn, Madonna's ballet mentor, took an ugly turn eventually—ending many years later with his death from AIDS. Madonna's brother Christopher would take another path and eventually become Madonna's right-hand assistant on her world tours.

But that was all far in the future.

3

NEW YORK, NEW YORK!

Madonna was only seventeen and a high school graduate in 1976. Because of her excellent grade point average in high school, she won a four-year scholarship to the University of Michigan in Ann Arbor— a four-year course in the Dance Department.

Being ambitious, Madonna had enrolled in a six-week dance course at Duke University in Durham, North Carolina, to sharpen up her moves before entering the university. There was nothing particularly spectacular about the course; she simply learned what she could from it.

But one of the perquisites fascinated her. Anyone who attended Duke was given a free tryout for a scholarship to study in New York with two top choreographers. They were the late Alvin Ailey and Pearl Lang, unquestionably the best dancers of their time.

So it was that at the age of seventeen Madonna packed up her dancing shoes and other paraphernalia in a suitcase, put thirty-five dollars in her bag, threw in a giant baby doll as a security blanket along with a picture of her real mother— and flew to New York City.

"When I turned seventeen," was the way she put it, "I

moved to New York because my father wouldn't let me date boys at home. I never saw a naked body when I was a kid. Gosh, when I was seventeen, I still hadn't seen a penis!''

The move to New York, she later admitted, ''was the bravest thing I've ever done.'' With the brashness typical of Madonna's developing persona, she took a cab from the airport and instructed the driver, ''Take me to the middle of everything!''

The driver apparently took that to mean one thing only. ''Everything'' in the cabby's limited range of knowledge was Times Square—what else?— and soon Madonna found herself standing in the middle of the raunchiest section of the biggest city in the country staring about her in disbelief and some concern.

''When you're only seventeen, New York can be a very overwhelming place. Nothing will ever surpass that moment for shock value!''

The story goes that as she walked eastward along Forty-Second Street and then south on Lexington Avenue, completely out of place in the hot summer weather, lugging her suitcase and wearing a warm winter coat, a curious male stranger began following her. Finally he smiled and made his move.

''Hello! Why are you walking around with a winter coat and a suitcase?''

''I just got off the plane,'' Madonna told him.

''Why don't you go home and get rid of them?''

''I don't live anywhere.''

Within minutes Madonna was telling him her entire life story, and he was listening with a funny smile on his face. Finally he said, ''Well, you can stay at my apartment.''

Madonna was naive enough to take him at his word. She moved in!

Oddly enough, it worked out fine. The punch line was that nothing really happened to shock her or to defeat her in her main purpose in coming to New York.

''I stayed there for the first two weeks,'' she said. ''He didn't try to rape me or anything. He showed me where everything was and he gave me breakfast. It was perfect.''

The transitional period was tough, but Madonna rose above any problems that surfaced.

"I took to New York straight away, but I was really lonely. I would take whatever I could take in a taxicab, to wherever I could go to next. I'd take a big breath, grit my teeth, blink back my tears, and say, 'I'm going to do it; I have to do it, because there's nowhere else for me to go.'"

Her brashness and self-confidence carried her right through the audition that she had been promised with Alvin Ailey and Pearl Lang. In fact even before the audition began, Madonna strolled over to the table at the head of the room where several of the judges were seated. She announced to one of them, "I'm auditioning for this scholarship so I can work with Pearl Lang. I saw one of her performances, and she's the only one I want to work with."

The woman stared right back at her, brash for brash. "Of course," she said. "Allow me to introduce myself," she told Madonna with a faint smile. "I'm Pearl Lang. And you're—?"

"Madonna's eyes almost came out of her head," Lang recalled with a laugh.

In the event, Madonna did impress the judges enough to be chosen as one of the six dancers in the country to be awarded a scholarship to Alvin Ailey's New York studio.

The work was hard, the learning experience was endless, and the days faded into the nights. But the world of dance was the place Madonna wanted to be. Pearl Lang was one of the grandes dames of modern dance, one of the lead soloists of the famous Martha Graham Dancers. At that time she was artistic director for the Alvin Ailey Studio.

Lang recently recalled Madonna as a "remarkable individual."

"She was an exceptional dancer," Lang said. "Many dancers can kick and exhibit acrobatic body control, but that is just run-of-the-mill, taken for granted. Madonna had the power, the intensity, to go beyond mere physical performance into something far more exciting. That intensity is the first thing I look for in a dancer, and Madonna had it."

In fact, Lang added, "Madonna simply *has* the magical quality that a great artist needs."

Madonna lasted out the course and returned home safely to Michigan. She reactivated her scholarship to the University of Michigan and enrolled in the fall. At Ann Arbor she did everything she could do to call attention to herself. She wore her hair in a spiky punk haircut. She ripped apart her leotards and pinned the parts together again with safety pins. She danced in a bra rather than a leotard during the hot summer months. She cultivated the obnoxious habit of belching out loud in class.

"I was a real ham," she confessed. "I did everything I could to get attention, to stand out from the others." The idea was to proclaim to the world, "I'm not like you. Okay? I'm taking dance classes and everything, but I'm not stuck here."

Actually Madonna was deliberately fine-tuning her dance techniques. She had no serious intention of staying at Michigan any longer than she had to. And in the long run she stuck to her resolve. She was preparing herself for splitsville, in the jargon of the time.

In high school Madonna had looked down on her peers. Her attitude had not changed a bit; if anything, it had intensified by the time she got to the University of Michigan. She considered the other students at the university "bratty little girls who stared at themselves in the mirror all day."

For all her competitive aggressiveness, she won only muted disapproval and actually aroused envy of the worst kind in her peers. They all hated her. Because of course they were not as good as she was.

At night she took to visiting nightclubs near the university. She still loved to frequent haunts like that, to hear the music, to see the dancing, and to dance herself. She had become fascinated by nightlife in high school, had gone to these places with her dance instructor, Christopher Flynn, and was not about to give up that scene now.

One of the places she discovered in Ann Arbor was called the Blue Frogge. There she found that she could dance whenever she wanted to, to pass the time of night. She met a black waiter there—a tall, handsome, young man. His name, he told her, was Steve Bray. He was interested in music too. He played the drums. He sang. He wrote lyrics. He waited on tables just to earn enough money to live on. Naturally.

"He was really cute," Madonna once told a *Rolling Stone* interviewer, "all soulful and funky. First time in my life I asked a guy to buy me a drink."

She began following the local band, of which Bray was a member in his off hours. Occasionally she would jump up onstage to dance with one of the group. Bray himself was much taken with Madonna. "She stood out," he said. "Her energy was really apparent."

The romance went on for a time—for it *was* a romance—but, like Madonna's college career at Ann Arbor, it was short-lived. Madonna was only three semesters into her college career when she decided that she was simply spinning her wheels hanging around in Michigan. Spinning the wheels that she wanted to bite into the fast track of life far away in the Big Apple.

Quite unexpectedly, in 1978, Madonna was invited to take classes with the Alvin Ailey troupe's third company, meaning that she would be studying *and* performing on the road simultaneously. The third company was a far cry from the *first* company obviously. At most it was a modest step upward. But Madonna had never looked back before. She did not intend to now.

"I'm going to New York for good," she told her father after receiving the offer from the Ailey troupe. He was appalled and tried to argue her out of the move. He wanted her to get a college education the way he had. His pleas did little good.

Steve Bray also did not want Madonna to leave Michigan.

"Looking back," said Madonna, "I think that I probably did make Steve feel kind of bad, but I was really insensitive in those days. I was totally self-absorbed."

Even though she was working in dance, she was not making money at it in Michigan. New York was never a free ride for her, or for anyone else, for that matter. She needed to earn enough money at least to pay for basic food and shelter. She determined that, as hard as that might be, she would support herself while she moved up in the world of dance.

She got herself a cheap place in a slum area on East Fourth

Street on the Lower East Side—232 East Fourth Street. "When my father came to visit, he was mortified," Madonna recalled with sardonic amusement. "The place was crawling with cockroaches. There were winos in the hallways, and the entire place smelled like stale beer."

There were, however, compensations to living in the area. There were blacks there, and Hispanics—people with whom Madonna felt a complete rapport—and the graffiti on the buildings was reminiscent of the seamier sections of the big cities in Michigan. Besides, these people all had the right attitude—they were hip, streetwise, and with it. She thrived on the life.

For income Madonna landed a job at the Dunkin' Donuts across the street from Bloomingdale's big department store in uptown Manhattan. Later she moved up a notch or two—or perhaps sideways—when she got a job at a Burger King, and then later at a Greek chain called Amy's. Once, she hit the big time by working as a hatcheck girl at the famous Russian Tea Room. But these jobs were hard work.

There was an easier way to make good money. . . .

"I started modeling for a lot of art schools, for the drawing and painting classes." That meant she was posing in the nude for artists of all kinds. "Because I was a dancer, I was in really good shape, and I was slightly underweight, so you could see my muscle definition and my skeleton. I was one of their favorite models because I was easy to draw."

As for her social life: "I used to go out with graffiti artists," she said. "I got in the habit of carrying markers and writing my name everywhere."

In this phase of her social life Madonna met a man named Norris Burroughs. She even began dating him. Burroughs had become well known as the "king" of the graffiti T-shirt designers in Manhattan. For three months their romance ran from friendship to dating to living together.

In the end it was not Madonna who broke off the relationship but Burroughs. He had found himself another woman. Burroughs compensated, however, by introducing Madonna to a good friend of his named Dan Gilroy. Gilroy was a sometime painter, sometime writer, sometime musician.

Burroughs worked both sides against the middle. He built

up Gilroy to Madonna and built up Madonna to Gilroy. When they finally met, the relationship almost fizzled from the start from overexposure and what Charles Dickens might have termed too-great expectations on both sides.

For himself Gilroy was not entranced with Madonna. "At the party [where we met] she was wearing these clothes that looked like a clown outfit," he recalled. "She didn't make a huge impression on me at first because she seemed sort of draggy, like depressed—or something."

That was part of Madonna's self-confessed "killjoy" characteristic. It turned Gilroy off; he was not entranced.

But Madonna was not going to let any opportunity pass her by. She began circling about Gilroy, looking at him, sizing him up, and wondering about him. At the windup of the evening she finally walked right up to him, stood in front of him, turned her chin up, and asked him, "Aren't you going to kiss me?"

What could Gilroy do? Turn down an offer like that? Or was it an offer? Wasn't it more of a command?

Whatever—command performance or not—he kissed her. What male wouldn't?

After the kiss, Gilroy remembered, "When I kissed Madonna, it was wonderful. I melted." And because he melted, that impression of her remained engraved on his memory. Later he could recall to the detail what she was wearing that night—the tatty outfit that at first had turned him off.

"[It was] a kind of circus outfit, very short with a blue tutu, and dark-blue leggings. And she had olive oil in her hair, which made it quite strange and matted. It was influenced by punk, but she was moving in her own direction.

"It was quite weird, really, because she was just kind of sitting there and she seemed depressed—I think she'd come to the party with someone she didn't want to be with. So I was her dancing partner, and we hit it off and got together."

Forgotten were the moves Burroughs had put on Gilroy to impress him with Madonna. Forgotten were the first negative impressions he had gotten of her. Madonna did that to men she wanted to impress: made them forget everything but her.

Dan Gilroy was doing a two-man comedy act with his

brother, Ed, at the time he met Madonna. Called *The Bil and Gil Show,* it was a mildly successful attraction around the circuit. The brothers lived in Corona, Queens—across the East River from Manhattan—and they had fixed up an abandoned synagogue, which they used as a bedroom and as a studio. The neighborhood was the usual eclectic miscellany of black, Hispanic, Italian, Jewish, and even Oriental.

When Dan Gilroy announced to his brother, Ed, that Madonna was going to move in with them, there was no resistance. In fact Madonna returned to music when she moved in with the Gilroys—music that she had abandoned deliberately many years before in Michigan when she had dropped the piano lessons her father had forced her to take. Now she found herself surrounded by musical instruments of all kinds in the studio in Corona.

Gilroy saw her looking the items over and stuck a guitar in her hand. "He tuned it to an open chord so that I could strum it," Madonna said. "That really clicked something off in my brain." So, in that simple manner Madonna was reunited with music. And she began to sing once more.

Pearl Lang took note of her sudden interest in music, but did not realize it might eventually supplant her interest in dancing.

"She had taken up singing," Pearl Lang said of Madonna's early transition to music. "But I never took much notice of it. I believe that at that time even she was unaware of how far she would take it."

Madonna was beginning to look beyond the dance world into the world of music and song—that larger world of which dance was simply part and parcel. And Madonna was encountering for the first time one of the main obstacles in the careers of hundreds of dancers: There were too many good competitors in the dance world, with not enough dance companies to accommodate them all.

In Madonnaese she was getting sick of working her ass off for nothing.

While singing with *The Bil and Gil Show* she began to make the rounds of the multimedia rock/vaudeville show circuit. And, oddly enough, that led to a strange but major break for her.

"Once I felt really confident about my dancing," Madonna explained, "I went into music. I started writing songs, but when I had to get out in front of lots of people and actually perform for them, I encountered all the same fears of awkwardness and uncertainty that I felt when I first started dancing.

"Every time I start something new, my knees tremble, and I want to learn. I'm afraid, and I'm also excited. I'm just like an open book. I want to get everything into my head that I can, then get it out."

In 1979 Madonna cut back her dancing classes to one a day and started looking for work in earnest in the singing field.

"I wanted to make more of my assets, you might say, so I decided to audition for the musical theater. I'd turn up at auditions and tell them I could dance and sing, because I wanted to use my voice."

Leafing through the trade papers as she had grown accustomed to do ever since arriving in New York, Madonna one day found that a "revue" group was looking for singers and dancers for a projected world tour. The revue was fronted by a German singer named, inappropriately enough, Patrick Hernandez. Hernandez was a disco singer who had made it on the rather slim talent exhibited in a disco song titled "Born to Be Alive," which nevertheless had become a huge international best-seller.

Madonna decided to try out for the group.

The rest, as one might truthfully say about this particular audition, was *not* history.

But it was a turning point.

4
City of Light

Patrick ("Born to Be Alive") Hernandez was unfortunately exactly what he had been built up to be in the eyes of those who viewed his lumbering Las Vegas–type show—a strutting, ponderous, overacting ham.

Gritting her teeth, Madonna appeared at the audition and sang for a number of narrow-eyed cynics dressed in business suits and seated in various parts of the auditorium. Although she was not aware of it, two of these plump middle-aged Babbitts, who might have been typecast as Mafiosi in a *film noir* of the 1940s, were actually French citizens.

Their names were as impressive as their weights: Jean Claude Pellerin and Jean Van Lieu. More impressive than names *or* weight was the fact that they were the invisible puppeteers who controlled the movements of the German with the Spanish-Irish name. They were the producers of the *Patrick Hernandez Revue*.

Madonna performed the audition with a somewhat ho-hum attitude: I've done it; it's not their thing; maybe next time. And therefore she was pleasantly surprised to be telephoned some days after the tryout and told to come in for a discussion with Messieurs Pellerin and Lieu. The wording of the invitation was obviously intended to inform her that she had not made it for the world tour, but . . .

And, sure enough, when Madonna showed up to meet the two Frenchmen, they told her immediately, "We don't want you to do the revue."

"What *do* you want me to do?" Madonna asked, looking them straight in the eye.

One of them repeated the immortal film cliché, second only to "Let's do a show!": "We want to make you a star!"

Madonna blinked. She couldn't *believe* it. But she played it straight.

Actually it was no bluff. The producers explained to her that their production company was based in Paris, with international contacts for tours everywhere. What they wanted Madonna to do was to join them and travel back with them to Paris. There, they promised, they would hire a vocal coach for her and train her to sing while they searched for the proper material for her act. After all, they had made "Born to Be Alive" Hernandez an international star. What couldn't they do for Madonna?

"They were offering me a lot of money and a recording contract," Madonna said. "I'd never been abroad before and I wanted to see a bit of the world."

She agreed to go to Paris in a month. Then, when she got back to the Gilroys' place, she had to break the news to Dan Gilroy.

"When you know a relationship isn't meant to last," Gilroy said later, "you can make each moment as intense as you want." He took it in stride, and the two of them let out all the stops and enjoyed themselves to the fullest in that short magic time before the jetliner took off for Paris with Madonna in it.

Paris was—

The greatest experience of Madonna's life?

The best thing that ever happened to her?

One gorgeous, romantic adventure?

The be-all and end-all of life?

No.

Paris was, in the words of Madonna, "Hey, like a French movie."

Why not?

It was all new to her. She reveled in the quaintness of the outdoor cafés. She exulted in the illuminated Eiffel Tower at midnight. She prowled the marvelous book stands along the Seine.

In short she fell under the spell of Paris, as any American would.

But . . .

Like most Americans, Madonna was not a natural linguist. The French language represented a tangle of incomprehensibility to her, as it does to most other Yankees. But the Parisians she met were bilingual or multilingual—and communication was not the main snag. Her mentors, Les Deux Jeans, did everything they could to help her orient herself to the life they loved and surmised that she would love once she got used to it.

True to their promise, they hired a team of experts to groom Madonna for stardom on an international level. They set her up in a luxury apartment with a maid and a private chauffeur—including a huge limousine to lumber around Paris in. They mounted plans to feature her in several of their television shows; they had connections everywhere and produced a few of the biggest shows on French TV.

All that was in the offing.

What actually the experts came up with was a song for Madonna, tailor-made for her, Les Deux Jeans said, titled "She's a Real Disco Queen."

Nothing came of it. *Rien* (read: zip).

Meanwhile Madonna was making the rounds of all the "right places" in Paris. She hit the chic restaurants and night-clubs and went to all the "in" parties. Les Deux Jeans introduced her to dozens of suntanned, handsome, hip, lithe, and rich French youths. What should have become the French connection of the decade became more a kind of French disconnection, or unconnection.

There was simply no rapport. She did not thrive in the City of Light. Stuck-up Parisian aristocrats who spent the winter on the Riviera getting tanned, drunk, and serviced were not the kind of people Madonna longed to be with. Where were the neighborhood kids? Where were *her* people? So, Madonna did exactly what she should have been expected to do. She curled her upper lip at them and made her demands on Les Deux Jeans.

First she demanded money.

Oddly enough, they gave it to her!

Yet, there was no change in her static situation. She sat in her posh apartment like a lonely kid, miserable and aching to get back to work. Madonna's best therapy had always been hard work. She needed it now. But there was no work now to do. She was being given everything. Everything in Paris was—face it—nothing.

Then gradually Madonna unraveled the plot and deduced what was *really* in the minds of Les Deux Jeans. What they had schemed from the beginning was to develop a Madonna of their own making. The scenario they had dreamed up would create their own private international Madonna. She would be nothing more than a mannikin to their Frankensteinian vision, thus:

The story line would be that these producers had discovered a marvelously talented waif in the garbage-strewn streets of decadent New York, had rescued her, and brought her to Paris, where they were going to create a brand-new Edith Piaf out of—out of nothing!

The scenario read good. It was a hell of a plot—and it would have worked in the milieu in which Les Deux Jeans were working.

But *they* would be the controllers of Madonna's destiny. And the role Madonna would be playing was herself—but a *fake* herself!

"Once again I was forced into the role of *enfant terrible*," Madonna said. "All I wanted to do was make trouble, because they stuck me in an environment that didn't allow me to be free." Or to get to work, which was what she really wanted to do. So, she altered the action of their brilliant story slightly and developed her own role within the concept they had dreamed up.

With the money they gave her to shop for glamorous "disco" duds, she bought black jeans, jack boots, and black leather jackets.

"I had my ears pierced and put safety pins in them," she

said. "And when they gave me more money, I ran out and went riding on the motorbikes of those low-life Vietnamese and Algerian boys."

These rough bikers were her kind of people, Madonna discovered. By connecting with them instead of the high-class Parisian aristocrats, Madonna was making her own statement—or at least giving the lie direct to the image created by Les Deux Jeans.

With the bikers she began riding through the streets of Paris, terrorizing the staid and sophisticated citizens of the City of Light and causing looks of horror on the faces of the gendarmes.

To more or less try to hold her in line, Les Deux Jeans finally agreed to let Madonna join the *Patrick Hernandez Revue* on its trip to Tunisia. Tunisia was at least an exotic country, although not as French as she had anticipated it to be. Besides, show-biz people were treated there like show-biz types in most European countries—probably two or three rungs down the ladder from the lowest servants on the social totem pole.

By the time Madonna returned with the troupe from Tunisia, she had really had just about enough of her Parisian adventure. And in the mail she got some letters from none other than Dan Gilroy, a man who did not write letters as a normal thing.

"He was my saving grace," Madonna said. "His letters were so funny. He'd paint a picture of an American flag and write over it, like it was from the president."

"We miss you," he wrote. "You must return to America."

About her Parisian interlude Madonna once summed it up: "They took me to Paris to make me the next Edith Piaf. They made me meet those awful French boys, and I would throw tantrums. They would just laugh and give me money to keep me happy."

Now she was ready to go back to New York.

And then, suddenly, out of the blue, she was a very sick woman. She had developed pneumonia somehow—from some bug caught in Tunisia perhaps, or even in the streets of Paris with the Vietnamese—and she was hospitalized by a worried pair of French producers.

Nevertheless she was ministered to by the very best in French physicians and looked after by swarms of nurses and nurses' aides. Yet, she was surprisingly slow in recovering. Finally at the end of her sickness, she begged Les Deux Jeans for a travel holiday. They gave it to her.

"I hadn't signed any contracts," Madonna said, "so I just left everything I had there and never returned. As far as actual productive musical stuff, I had nothing to show for the six months I had spent there."

It was not easy getting settled back in New York, but by now Madonna had friends there. She did not want to move in with the Gilroys again—even if they had asked her to. Instead she moved into a Lower East Side building with another friend, an illustrator named Martin Burgoyne.

However, the neighborhood was under siege, and when a gang of kids ransacked an adjacent apartment, Madonna fled over to Abbie Hoffman's old digs on Thirteenth Street. Burgoyne decided to tough it out on the East Side, but within forty-eight hours his apartment was trashed by toughs, who left chicken droppings all over the place. Some kind of exotic voodoo rite. He joined Madonna on Thirteenth Street.

Welcome back to the Big Apple!

Madonna told the Gilroys that while she was in France, she had decided to concentrate on rock music rather than on dance. If she could get herself up as a singer, she could join them and perform with them!

"I had this theory," Dan Gilroy said, "that anyone with a sense of timing could be a drummer. So, when Madonna came back with the music bug, I began teaching her how to play drums."

Gilroy's brother, Ed, was ready to show Madonna the basics of the rhythm guitar. Three people weren't really enough, they thought, to form a group, so Madonna invited a dancer friend of hers to join them; her friend, Angie Smit, promised to practice on the bass guitar in return for getting the job.

"Madonna was a maniac for rehearsing," Gilroy recalled. "Rehearse, rehearse, rehearse—she's a real workaholic. We'd rehearse all night and into the morning, then we'd all go out for breakfast."

Breakfast would be at the local International House of Pancakes. And so the band found its new name: Breakfast Club.

By now the Gilroys had invited Madonna back to the loft in Corona, and she spent all the time practicing on her drums when the two Gilroys were out.

"I became an excellent drummer," Madonna said. "I was really strong and I'd had all this dance training, so I had all this energy. Instead of dancing eight hours a day, I was practicing the drums for four hours a day. I drove everybody mad!"

Soon Madonna was working on the guitar, with Gilroy teaching her how to play chord progressions. And she even began tinkering with the piano keyboard again, experimenting with music. "It was an intensive musical training, but I was full of energy and raring to go."

Once she had accumulated a bit of musical knowledge, she began writing her own songs, taking up once again her adolescent interest in expressing words and ideas. And as she wrote the songs, she began to improve her control over the words she used to express the emotions.

Slowly and unconsciously Madonna began to take over the leadership of the group, and soon she was running the whole show in an overt and foreordained manner. It was her energy that kept them all going.

Gilroy remembered, "She'd be up in the morning. She'd have a quick cup of coffee and then sit by the phone and call up everybody—everyone from local record dealers to potential management."

"I took advantage of the situation," Madonna admitted. "I wanted to know everything they knew, because I knew I could make it work to my benefit. It was one of the happiest times of my life. I really felt loved. Sometimes I'd write some sad songs and [Dan Gilroy] would sit there and cry. Very sweet."

The Breakfast Club began getting jobs—on the Lower East Side. There was one problem from the onset. It was the fourth member, Angie Smit.

"For one," Gilroy recalled, "Angie would hardly play any

music live. After all our rehearsals her performance consisted mainly of standing there staring at the audience. *Occasionally* she might play a note or two."

In addition to Smit's freeze-frame stance, she presented a costuming problem. Gilroy once described her dress as "several strings of beads loosely sewed together," and "something like a chain-link fence."

The effect was to induce the audience to gawk at Smit's rather appealing dancer's body, which was revealed in almost all its subtleties, distracting attention from the group and its music and focusing all eyes directly on her.

"People looked at us like a strip show," Gilroy said.

Obviously Madonna was well aware of the attention Smit was getting, along with the reason for it. It was, Madonna realized, not an *undressed* person who was getting the attention, but a *revealing* person in the *way* she dressed herself. This registered with Madonna. She was learning something she herself would use later.

It was not easy to persuade Smit to leave the group, but the Gilroys were persistent, and finally there were just three of them left in the Breakfast Club. Now Madonna began working on Dan Gilroy to write songs for her to sing. Finally he told her he would let her try one.

When he did, she began to practice her singing, and it was not long before she took over as the group's principal singer. In a way it was a surprise. Madonna was not a natural singer. She was shaky and insecure. Singing was not dancing—it was much more a conscious art than something that came from within. She did not seem to have the built-in talent for it.

The first time she stepped out from behind her drums and moved to the center of the stage, she found herself on the verge of fainting. As soon as she began singing, however, she lost her self-consciousness and found that she could sing as well as she could dance.

By now the Breakfast Club was beginning to look like a disjointed replica of its former self. Madonna would bang away at the drums for a few numbers, and then she would come out from behind the drums, take the mike, and sing a couple of songs. The group clicked for a while, but it became obvious to the patrons that the Breakfast Club was a schizoid combination that simply did not come together in any fashion.

It was, in show-biz parlance, a two-act partnership that competed with itself for attention.

"I was just a lot more goal-oriented and commercial than they were," Madonna said later, analyzing the problem.

She was unhappy, but resolved to continue in her own fashion. "I knew that Dan and Ed were afraid that I was going to steal all the attention, so I thought to myself, 'I'm going to have to leave and front my own band.' "

And she did.

"I miss her very much," Gilroy said. "It had been a good year. Having Madonna there had been a bonus."

He was philosophical about the split.

"There was the normal separation anxiety of course," he said. "But I think we both knew our relationship didn't have a feeling of permanence in it."

5

John Lennon Redivivus

In early 1980 Madonna was on her own in the strange business of professional musicianship. Prior to this time she had existed professionally as part of some larger group controlled by someone else. It was strange, but not unpleasant, to find herself the lead singer and true head of an entire musical aggregation.

Although she had always subconsciously considered herself the leader of any group she was a part of, she had habitually submerged herself below the level of one or several others, more or less as the programmed reaction of a woman born into a macho-oriented Catholic family.

By rising above the level of all others in the group, she now found herself the unwitting target of every gripe, complaint, and otherwise denigrating commentary about the group's performance. She soon began to work out a satisfactory method of dealing with the widely touted problem of loneliness at the top. She simply ignored it.

Madonna rented a garage in Queens and set it up as a rehearsal hall. Meeting with a rather ill-assorted bunch of backup musicians, Madonna decided to call the group Emmenon, later modified to Emmy. *Emmena*, incidentally, is classical Greek for "menses." From the beginning Emmy was hard work, long hours, and frustration.

As lead singer and lead guitarist Madonna soon learned the basic lesson of show biz: Loyalty is a thing spelled C.A.S.H. The engagements were at first few and far between. After each gig Madonna found that she had to replace an errant sideman or two—sometimes the entire bunch. Musicians without contracts, she found, were equivalent to mercenary soldiers; they simply signed up at all times with the highest bidder.

One of her first faithful drummers was Mike Monahan, but he soon married and left the group to get an honest job to support his family. Ironically, at just about the time of Monahan's defection, Madonna received a communiqué from none other than Steve Bray in Michigan. Bray told Madonna that he had about decided to pack it in in Michigan and move his skins and himself to New York. Madonna immediately invited him to join Emmy.

"I found that, oddly enough, she needed a drummer," said Bray. "So I said, 'Fine, I'll be there next week.' " That, despite the fact that they had had their troubles in the past. When Bray arrived, the two settled down to some hard work together. They began writing songs and set up long rehearsal schedules.

Soon Madonna was able to book Emmy into some run-down, very low-class New York clubs. Actually Emmy was only given the dregs of the engagements. Most of the time they would be lucky to earn twenty-five dollars a night. The big money was simply not there.

Although Bray toughed it out with Madonna, the rest of the group was on a permanently impermanent basis. Last in, first out. And so on.

The story went that Madonna and Bray worked out a budget plan: one dollar a day for food. The "food" turned out to be yogurt and peanuts at the local Korean delicatessens.

"There were always garbage cans," Madonna recalled. "If there was a Burger King bag sitting on top that someone had just deposited, I'd open it up, and if I was lucky, there'd be some French fries that hadn't been eaten. I'm a vegetarian."

It was not the best of times. Actually, to vivisect Dickens, it was the worst of times. The gigs were few and far between. And then one night Madonna woke up in the loft where she lived. It was so cold in the place that she had surrounded her mattress on the floor with a number of cheap electric heaters, all focused in on her.

Blinking, she tried to get a grasp on what was happening. Finally she realized that she was surrounded by flames. The carpet under one of the heaters had caught fire. The fire was dancing up and down all around her.

"I jumped up and dumped water everywhere, which only made it spread more. Then my nightgown caught fire."

She tore it off, grabbed her clothes, and ran out of the loft, phoning in the alarm to the fire department on the way out.

 Success was not there for Emmy—or for Madonna as singer/leader of a musical group. As a desperation measure she turned once again to a more lucrative source of income. She returned to modeling in the nude.

"I ended up modeling privately in people's houses," Madonna said. "I got to know the artists in a friendly kind of way. They became like surrogate mothers and fathers, and they took care of me.

"I also got involved with photographers. I consider the nude [photograph] a work of art. I really don't see pornography in Michelangelo."

 Eventually her friends started recommending her to photographers who were doing exhibits of nude pictures. Photography sessions paid a great deal more than posing for drawings. "It's for art," Madonna thought. It was largely through her work in this esoteric "nudie" field that Madonna was able to add a new dimension to her image, which by now consisted of singer, musician, and dancer. The new dimension was her image on a photograph.

 Leafing through the trades again, Madonna read that a film writer/director was interested in new faces for various projects he had in the works. In fact the man was searching for the lead in what appeared to be—couched in the basically ambivalent prose of the usual advertisement of that kind—the lead role in an "art film."

Madonna's approach was novel. She wrote a two-page letter by hand and sent with it an assortment of snapshots. Stephen Jon Lewicki, the "writer/director" who had written the original ad, was interested. Madonna's handwritten effusion stood out from the standard typed résumé and professional head shots that lay all over his desk.

"Her approach was strange," he said later. "Very strange. But I decided to follow it up."

He called her on the telephone.

The conversation was an odd one, according to Madonna's memory. Lewicki set up a meeting with her, not in an office of any kind but in the middle of Washington Square Park—the large green common at the start or finish of Fifth Avenue, whichever way one looks at it. Even at that time Washington Square was, as it is now, a notorious drug exchange.

Although Madonna did not know him at all, she agreed to meet him, even in those most inauspicious surroundings. As soon as she met him, she found out about his background. A philosophy major from Columbia University, Lewicki had switched careers and taken up filmmaking at New York University Film School.

A brilliant, innovative man, he was in his final year there now. He had evolved a uniquely personal method of auditioning—and of making—films. He believed absolutely in the integrity and inviolability of the personal one-on-one conversation, as opposed to readings, run-throughs, or performances of any kind.

In his eyes Madonna was an amazingly personable woman who had an innocence and vulnerability that shone through her obvious streetwise and assertive personality.

"From the moment I met her," Lewicki said, "I knew she was a star. She fit the role perfectly and had a riveting personality. She has the charisma that makes a star a star."

He hired here then and there, on the spot on that bench in Washington Square, over some hundred other applicants. Instantly Madonna became a certified member of the cast. She was incidentally the only one who was selected as a result of an audition/conversation with Lewicki. The others had all been referred to Lewicki by actors, writers, and producers he knew.

Actually Madonna was to be paid one hundred dollars for acting the lead in a picture called *A Certain Sacrifice*—a film that might be euphemistically described as an avant-garde, underground film. Truthfully it was a kind of sadomasochistic piece of low-budget soft porn.

Her role in the film was that of Bruna, a young woman living in New York, doing just about what she pleases in her life, who falls in love with a young man named Dashiel. The action concerns first of all the rape of Bruna by an older man and the subsequent revenge motif supplied by Bruna to motivate her young man to track down the rapist and kill him.

In spite of the corny elements of melodrama in the story line and the plot clichés involved, the role provided certain tricky scenes for Madonna to work out. It was an exciting thing for her to do the role at all. Madonna realized that she was now going to be a full-fledged professional screen actress. Even if she was acting in a piece of sludge.

Independent Film & Video Monthly called the picture "a bizarre story of urban terror." Madonna looked back on the adventure some years later and admitted that the film was "real stupid and hilarious," and indeed was actually a "very sick" film.

Her description of the plot added in a few more details that tended to reveal the film was something close to or not far from soft porn: "It was sick in a childish kind of way. It's about this girl in post-punk New York called Bruna, who's a dominatrix—me of course. There's hardly any sex scenes, it's just implied all the time. She's got love slaves and she leads this very perverted, deranged life. I get raped, which you don't see in the movie, and my boyfriend goes crazy with revenge, kills the guy, and performs this ritual sacrifice. There's a scene where we take a bath in fake blood."

Lewicki had a very different assessment of Madonna and her role. "Madonna is a very complex individual," he observed. "As an actress she is the consummate professional: on time, understands her role, always delivers her lines. But she has an incredible swing of moods in her personal life. She can express deep love, then fiery hatred for the same thing—or person—within a few minutes' time."

In spite of her own putdown of her film work, Madonna

did get a great deal of excellent acting exposure out of the job. What she learned would be difficult to detail, but certainly the work before the motion picture cameras would come in handy later on when for the first time she faced the cameras recording her singing, dancing, *and* acting for MTV!

Mainly Madonna was focusing now on writing songs and on singing and performing them. In 1981 she and Steven Bray rented rehearsal space in a run-down, ancient building in New York called the Music Building. In that building dozens of rock bands lived, rehearsed, and recorded their rock-and-roll offerings.

Madonna and Bray did not fit in with the crowds of rock musicians. A "big break" for the rockers would consist of getting steady employment at one of New York's broken-down rock clubs.

The dream Madonna had was different. She was going to break into the big time and become a national star. It was not in Madonna's makeup to keep this a secret from anyone, either. If anything, she believed in herself. And she believed in spreading the word about herself.

The rest of the crew that inhabited the Music Building came to loathe the two of them. The feeling was mutual.

"I thought they were all lazy," Madonna said. "I thought that only a handful of people were going to get out of that building to [go on to any] success."

Steve Bray remembered the ordeal of the Music Building somewhat differently. "There was a lot of resentment of someone who's obviously got that special something. [Madonna] had trouble making friends."

One day in the elevator Madonna rode up with a man whom she had never seen before. She was amused when she took a good close look at him. "Hey," she said, "you look like John Lennon."

The man, whose name was Adam Alter, grinned and asked her what her name was. She told him, and the two of them got to talking.

Alter had just formed a partnership with a woman named Camille Barbone in a rock management company they called Gotham Productions. Actually they were looking for rock-and-roll acts to manage and produce. One thing led to another in the conversation between Madonna and Alter, and finally Alter and Barbone agreed to listen to one of Madonna's demo tapes. The two of them were impressed.

"Right from the first," Alter recalled, "Camille and I were certain that Madonna was destined for great things. We wanted her to become a rock/pop multimedia superstar, appealing to everyone from little kids to adult theatergoers. To say we believed in her is an understatement. We signed her immediately."

In fact Camille Barbone and Madonna become firm friends. They discovered that they shared the same birthday, Camille being just eight years older than Madonna. Sharing a birthday or a zodiac sign was a big thing with Madonna—always—and would be an even bigger thing later on when she came to marry. Anyway Camille became a kind of surrogate mother to Madonna.

"I discovered that [Madonna] didn't have any money and hadn't eaten for three days," Barbone recalled. "She had a guitar, but the neck was broken. She had a bicycle, but that had a flat tire. I felt sorry for her; she was really in need."

When Madonna signed the contract with Gotham Management, she found that she could move out of the roach-infested rooming house where she lived—"a place filled with prostitutes, degenerates, and escaped convicts," in the words of Adam Alter—to share in an Upper West Side apartment.

Out of the deal with Gotham, Madonna got an apartment and a place to rehearse, both paid for by Gotham, as well as a salary of about a hundred dollars a week. She also got a catalog of musicians to choose from for her new band—all of whom would be paid by Gotham!

The only problem was Steve Bray. Madonna insisted that he be retained as her drummer. "Camille was against that," Alter said, "but Gotham—Camille and I—eventually agreed to it because we knew it would make Madonna happy."

Madonna and Camille Barbone grew so close that they became almost like daughter and mother. "I wanted to be the best manager in the world," Barbone said. "I became Madonna, and Madonna became me. If I could sing in another time and place, Madonna would have managed me. It's hard to talk about her and not sound in love with her. I guess I did love Madonna. I gave her everything."

In order to pump self-assurance into Madonna—something that she had never really had from the beginning—Barbone would praise her with a long shopping list of superlatives whenever she introduced her to anyone else. Alter tended to do the same thing.

"Sometimes I blame myself," Alter said. "Camille blames herself. Madonna was a very modest, humble girl when we met her, and the two of us treated her like a star before she was a star. Camille especially inflated her head with the star thing in a way that, in retrospect, was unbelievable."

Yet Gotham was not unsuccessful in booking Madonna's band, which was still using the name Emmy, into oddball clubs around New York such as Chase Park, Botany Talk House, and My Father's Place.

The music they played, according to Bray, was "really raucous rock and roll influenced by the Pretenders and the Police." In fact it was *not* the kind of pure funk that Madonna liked—or that she and Bray wanted to live by. The ambivalence was becoming noticeable. Two different music styles were on a collision course.

Gotham wanted Emmy to do commercial rock and roll. Madonna wanted to do streetwise downtown funk. But the gigs continued, and everything seemed on the upswing. Everything except the money. Gotham just wasn't making it as big as it *needed* to in order to succeed.

"We tried to get [Madonna] TV commercials and movie deals," Alter said. "But she didn't want to be bothered. At that time all she did was stay in the studio all day and write songs. She was turned off by any vision of herself except being a rock star." Actually Alter had it wrong. She wanted to be a funk star.

By 1981 Madonna seemed to have built up a small cult following in New York. But at the same time, as Madonna's image rose, the money in the Gotham till was draining out. After almost a year Madonna found herself with little more than she had begun with. To keep her under contract, Gotham

Management would have to make money fast.

Conflict erupted unexpectedly in personality clashes between Madonna and Camille Barbone. Steve Bray, who was witness to this break, explained it.

"If people felt exploited by Madonna—that's resentment of someone who's got drive. It seems like you're leaving people behind or you're stepping on them, and the fact is that you're moving and they're not. Madonna doesn't care if she ruffles someone's feathers."

The Gotham relationship was going sour. "I can be arrogant sometimes," Madonna admitted, "but I never meant it intentionally. I always acted like a star [long] before I was one."

"I made her cry," Barbone recalled. "I screamed at her and told her that she was a manipulative egomaniac who didn't give a damn about anyone. . . . She once provoked me to such a state of anger that I bashed my fists through a door and broke my wrist."

Alter understood Madonna's creative strengths and her personality weaknesses. "Like most good artists," he said, "she is very emotional. When she's sad or in a bad mood, she can't do anything. But get her in the right circumstances and she sets the studio on fire. That girl can write, sing, and perform hits."

But nothing seemed to be working out. Things were going bad with a vengeance.

6

THE GOTHAM TAPE

In the ensuing conflict between Madonna and Gotham Management, a demonstration tape that Gotham had financed and that Madonna and Bray had made became the central issue. The tape itself, which came to be known as *The Gotham Tape,* consisted of four songs. One of them was written by Camille Barbone.

The four songs were "I Want You" (Barbone's composition), "Society's Boy," "Love on the Run," and "Get Up."

"It all became a race," Alter observed. "The big race to get the big money by selling the tape. We had the star, we had the songs, and everything was right. The only problem was that there were too many egos clashing around. Everyone wanted a piece of Madonna."

The booking agents wanted their share. The talent scouts from major companies such as William Morris made promises coupled with demands. The bottom line of the whole mish-mash was that Gotham couldn't really get anyone to put it all together and seal it with a holographic kiss.

The big problem was—money. Lack of money.

"There were days," Alter said, "that I would go to the bank and there was nothing there. *Nothing.* It had all been spent promoting Madonna"—in spreading the word and in getting the bands together to make the demo tape.

If Gotham had nothing, what did Madonna have?

Madonna had exactly the same thing. Zip. She, too, had come up empty-handed. In fact, because of the weird contractual obligations included and the other contractual obligations *not* included, Madonna did not even own the tape with her four numbers on it.

"I suspect that nothing will ever happen with those early tapes," Alter said recently, "because the music industry overproduces so much that any tune in the slightest complication generally never makes it to radio land. Thousands of great tunes never get heard. It's sad but true that an artist like John Lennon had to die before we got to hear his early songs."

By 1982 Madonna was on the rise, and Gotham Management was in a free-fall. Something else was happening. The conflict between Madonna and Gotham—the difference in their approaches to music—was becoming more and more evident. Madonna and Bray were out on the town every night, making interesting discoveries. New York was gobbling up funk. It was the coming thing, it was here! It was on the radio stations. It was crashing out in the streets from the boomboxes carried around by the kids. It was everywhere—and Madonna and Bray loved it.

"I've always been into rhythmic music, party music, but Gotham wasn't used to that stuff, and although I'd agreed to do rock and roll, my heart was no longer in it," Madonna said. "Soul was my main influence, and I wanted my sound to be the kind of music I'd always liked. I wanted to approach it from a very simple point of view because I wasn't an incredible musician. I wanted it to be direct.

"I still loved to dance, and all I wanted to do was make a record that I would want to dance to and people would want to listen to on the radio."

Madonna wanted to do "more funky stuff." Finally she told Gotham, "Forget it, I can't do this anymore. I'm going to have to start all over."

And start all over she did. She left Gotham and went out on her own again. There was nothing Gotham could do to keep her.

"I lost everything," Madonna recalled bitterly. "My demo

tape was the property of Gotham Management." Well, yes—and no. Still, it was true that she did not *own* it herself. That was the main point.

She and Bray were virtually back on the street again. This was nothing new for Madonna—or for Bray. They would catch some sleep in the various studios they used to work in. Madonna began living in the same clothes, sometimes for days and weeks.

Meanwhile Bray would borrow keys to studios his friends were working in, and he and Madonna would go in and make tapes of new numbers they were working on. It was Madonna's firm intention to make a substitute tape for *The Gotham Tape*—one they could peddle around town.

As for *The Gotham Tape*, it passed into the possession of Media Sound, a studio that Gotham hired to record the four songs.

Soon enough, living from hand to mouth and stealing studio time with the help of their friends, Madonna and Bray worked up four numbers to take the place of the four on *The Gotham Tape*. The songs were "Everybody," "Burning Up," "Stay," and "Ain't No Big Deal."

With the new material Madonna started scouting around the town. To make herself noticed on the dance floors, she assembled a strange personal costume all her own: ripped-up net tops, out-of-shape lingerie and knitwear, and rubber and metal jewelry she begged off a French designer friend named Maripol.

In a way it was the beginning of Madonna's eclectic dressing style. While it was a kind of throwback to the type of dressing she had favored in high school and in college, it was *different*, and it did make her distinctly visible.

At the time the hottest place in the New York disco world was Danceteria. There a disk jockey named Mark Kamins was in full charge of whatever the dancers would dance to.

Kamins was an ex-A&R (artists and repertoire) man from one of the record companies. As a producer for Danceteria he was very up-front with what the dancers wanted. In addition he had record-company connections, having just finished producing a funk album for Capitol Records, largely on the strength of writing a novelty song used in it called "Snapshot."

Madonna, in her weird getup and her now-famous naked belly button in full cry, caught the eye of the disk jockey immediately. But whatever was in her mind, she did not make her move on him immediately. She took her own sweet time, understanding the male psychology intuitively.

KAMINS: I was spinning records at Danceteria. I've always been the DJ type—the kid who plays records at parties— and the moment I first got into a recording studio, I knew I wanted to be a *producer.* I was *always* looking for more record deals, something else to produce in the studio. Anyway there was a crowd at Danceteria that came every Saturday night just to dance. Madonna was special. She had her own style and a tremendous desire to *perform* for people. When she started tearing up the dance floor, there'd be twenty people getting up and dancing with her. She was innocent, ambitious, broke, and confused. She was living a hard life. One night she came up to the DJ booth and introduced herself.

MADONNA: I was flirting with him.

KAMINS: We started going out to clubs together. The upshot of it was that she gave me a tape she said she had made. It had four numbers on it.

MADONNA: The next day he played it over the speakers before the club opened.

KAMINS: God, it was good! I told her I was going to get her a record deal. I meant it.

MADONNA: He meant it, and he did.

Kamins was in contact with superscout Michael Rosenblatt, with whom Kamins had worked when Kamins was producing a dance record with David Byrne of Talking Heads. Rosenblatt was a rising young executive at Sire Records, owned by Warner Bros. Rosenblatt had earned his talent-scout spurs by recommending the B-52s, a white dance act, to Sire in 1977, when the industry buzzword was *punk.*

Rosenblatt remembered meeting Madonna. "Mark Kamins had told me that there was this incredibly attractive female singer that I should meet, so I took him up on his offer to introduce me to her. I was out on the town with the guys from Wham when all of our heads got turned around by this incredibly wild-looking, beautiful girl who was on her way up to the DJ booth. I immediately knew it was Madonna, introduced myself, and said, 'When you have your tape ready, I'd love to hear it.' "

Kamins worked with Madonna and Bray and finally got the tape up to quality and delivered it to Rosenblatt.

ROSENBLATT: I listened to the four cuts on the tape, then I rolled it back and listened to the first song again. That was enough for me.

Rosenblatt then turned to Madonna and asked her what she wanted to do with her life.

MADONNA: I want to make records.
ROSENBLATT (nodding): Then, let's go!

Before she left his office, Rosenblatt had drawn up a preliminary contract on a yellow legal pad outlining production costs, advance monies, and other expenses. In less than an hour from the time he had turned on the tape recorder, Kamins, Madonna, and Rosenblatt had agreed in principle on a solid record deal.

But there was one slight drawback.

The president of Sire Records was in the hospital. No deal with Sire Records could be finalized without the written approval of Seymour Stein, the man in the hospital.

Rosenblatt rushed over and played Madonna's tape for Stein that same afternoon. Stein then set up a meeting for the four of them—Rosenblatt, Kamins, Madonna, and himself—for the very next day.

"The minute I heard it," Stein remembered, "I knew she was special, so I called her up and asked her to come and see me next day."

Madonna had never heard of Seymour Stein, but he was

an eccentric music buff with a visionary instinct. And he was a man who made his moves more by ESP than by thoughtful analysis. He had to *see* Madonna and talk to her to get the *feel* of her.

"I had this idea that I was going to meet some really cold sort of person in a suit and tie," Madonna recalled.

"You know," Stein said, "you normally don't care what you look like when you're in a hospital. But I shaved, combed my hair. I even got a new dressing gown. From what I'd heard, I was excited to meet Madonna."

The scene in the hospital was unforgettable. Stein had completely forgotten to get into his brand-new dressing gown.

MADONNA: Here was this guy sitting there in his boxer shorts with a drip feed in his arm and goofing around. He had a big ghetto blaster sitting on the windowsill. He played my songs, right while I was there, in front of me, and he was saying, "It's great, it's great!", talking a mile a minute. I thought the guy was nuts, but he liked my music, so I wasn't going to complain.

STEIN: I knew—I just sensed—that there was something that set her apart. She was outgoing, strong, dynamic, and self-assured. I just wanted to rush right in and do a deal.

And do a deal he did. Stein signed her quickly to make three twelve-inch dance singles and offered her an advance of five thousand dollars.

MADONNA: What have I got to lose?

Nothing. She agreed. And she signed. It was her biggest break to date.

In its wake was another unresolved conflict. When she had signed the papers with Stein, she had also signed an agreement that Mark Kamins would produce her first record. That meant that Steve Bray, her longtime associate, was out in the cold. Bray would not be producing her first single, despite the fact that he had produced the tape that had gotten her the record deal.

"It was really awful," Madonna said, "but I just didn't trust him enough."

The details were never available, but it was known that Madonna and Bray had a bitter falling-out over what he considered as her betrayal of him. But, unbelievably, there was even more to come.

Kamins chose the instruments for the record, hired the musicians and the sound engineers, rented the studio, and oversaw all aspects of the musical production. But it was Rosenblatt who made the critical decision of what tunes would comprise Madonna's first single.

He selected "Everybody" as the B side—the flip side, in the parlance of the record business—and "Ain't No Big Deal," the song that was ultimately responsible for bringing about the record deal, as the number-one song.

Rosenblatt then outlined his scenario for the buildup and launching of Madonna as a singer. "Madonna is great," he said. "She will do anything to be a star, and that's exactly what I look for in an artist: *total* cooperation. I want that artist to be there to do whatever I need. Music is a business, after all, and I—my company—spend a fortune, literally, trying to break an act. It is imperative that the artist respect that investment. I try not to deal with artists who think, 'Music is fun: I can meet people, travel, and get laid a lot.'

"With Madonna I knew I had someone hot and cooperative, so I planned to build her career with singles rather than just put an album out right away and run the risk of disaster. Madonna is a unique talent in that she can sing, dance, and act, and she looks fabulous. Therefore I was able to do unique planning with her career, and it was incredibly satisfying to see all the pieces fall into place."

It was Rosenblatt who talked Warner Bros. into breaking a long-standing rule: no publicity on a single release unless it is part of an album. Because Rosenblatt wanted to ease Madonna into the mainstream with a single, he argued that the company should put up publicity money to help out.

Incidentally, at this point in her career the dark-haired Madonna had suddenly become a heavily bleached blonde.

All the publicity that was going to go out showed her as a blonde now rather than the brunette she had been a few weeks before.

In less than a month Madonna, Kamins, and the crew had finished up the two cuts for the first single in the studio and had their two songs ready. They took it over to Rosenblatt and the Warner Bros. brass. In silence Rosenblatt listened to the two songs: "Ain't No Big Deal," the lead, and "Everybody," the backup.

There was that murderous kind of dead silence at the end. Heavy tension. No one dared to breathe.

Rosenblatt shook his head. "Ain't No Big Deal" was a mistake, he said. For some reason the song had lost its vitality, its verve, in the current rendition. It also lacked commercial appeal—and Rosenblatt said simply that it would have to go.

What to do? Make another cut?

"It forced me to put 'Everybody' on both sides of the single," said Rosenblatt.

No matter.

"Everybody" launched Madonna immediately.

The scenario Rosenblatt had invented for starting Madonna included a special showcasing of the song at Danceteria in New York. Actually all she was required to do was to turn up and mime over a backup tape. However, Madonna decided to make a little more out of it than a simple lip-synched act. She got three dancers to back up her song, part of the No Entiendes (Spanish for "you don't understand") from Haoui Montang's Cabaret. They were Erica, Bogs, and Martin Burgoyne, at whose apartment Madonna had crashed after her flight from Paris.

Rosenblatt and Stein were in the audience as Madonna started her act. They did not know it, but her real ambition was to show Sire and Warner Bros. that she was worth a lot more than a three-single record deal.

"Everybody" met with big approval at Danceteria.

And elsewhere. All the dance-oriented radio stations in the country began picking up on it. The song was immediately in the Top Ten on the dance charts.

One odd detail that surfaced with Madonna's debut on

record was that the system of pigeonholing musical styles made it almost impossible to tag or label her subgenre. She was hailed as a New Wave disco artist, even though Madonna saw her song as "pop with a definite rhythm-and-blues sound." Oddly enough, the black programmers assumed she was a black singer because her voice had so much soul—a real tribute to the girl who had always considered herself more Motown than Bay City.

7

Jellybean

Madonna's personal life seemed to be in some kind of permanent stall. She had broken up with Steven Bray in the acrimonious confrontation over who would produce her first record. Mark Kamins had won that battle hands down. An off-again-on-again personal affair that she had just begun with Kenny Compton, an illustrator, was now more off than on.

But in Madonna's life there was always another man in her future. This time he turned out to be an in-house disc jockey at a disco called the Funhouse. His name was John Benitez, but everybody knew him as Jellybean. Jellybean came from the South Bronx; he was a Catholic, which proved to be an interesting switch for Madonna, who, in the past, had never favored men of her own religious turn.

Jellybean was attracted immediately to this up-and-coming—and extremely attractive—disco star.

"She was introduced to me by her record company," he recalled. "I thought she had a lot of style, and she crossed over a lot of boundaries, because everyone in the rock clubs played her—the black clubs, the gay, the straight. And very few records have *that* appeal."

As for Madonna, it really was not love at first sight with Jellybean, any more than it was instant rapport "across a crowded room" with Jellybean over Madonna.

"He took me around to all the DJs in the major clubs," she said of him. "They were places that were playing my records. He liked me, but nothing really happened in the beginning. We were both a bit cool."

Jellybean agreed to Madonna's assessment of their early relationship. "She didn't bowl me over at first. We just used to go to the movies and clubs together. Then we started holding hands and buying each other presents."

It was an easy relationship to slip into, and the two of them let it all happen with a minimum of fuss and feathers.

Meanwhile Madonna was packing them into the New York discos, where she appeared—and where her record was being played. With "Everybody" suddenly Number Three, Warner Bros. began to take some notice of what it might have in Madonna.

And work began moving ahead in the first months of 1983 to do another single and perhaps prepare a debut album for this potentially big new star. There was, in fact, enough interest in her for the company to think of plowing serious money into promoting her.

Nevertheless an album was a risky venture. It *had* to be right. And that meant that production values as well as creative values had to be on the mark. Once again Madonna was faced with a painful decision. Would the album be produced by Mark Kamins, who had produced her first single? Would it be produced by Steve Bray, who had been aced out as producer of her debut single?

Somehow it was not quite so simple as that.

From the beginning Madonna knew that she would rise or fall on the quality of her debut album. She knew that both Steve Bray and Mark Kamins were in line for the job. However, she also knew that both men were relatively inexperienced in the album field and might blow the job. It was a typical Madonna dilemma: two one-time boyfriends vying for a most important job in her career.

There was of course a third factor—the kicker. Madonna

saw it clearly, even if Bray and Kamins did not. The third factor was Madonna's career itself. And *that* was riding on the skill and technical virtuosity of whoever produced the album. Madonna knew where her future lay. She knew what she had to tell not only Bray but Kamins as well.

"I was really scared," she recalled. "I felt I had been given a golden egg with this album and I just didn't trust Steve enough to produce it. I said he could play the instruments, but he didn't believe in the ethics of the situation. It was really awful."

Bray and Madonna had had falling-out over the first single, anyway, but they were still in touch. But now—

"It was very hard to accept at the time," Bray said. And this time he acted. He split with her professionally to join another group that was still performing—a group that Madonna had interesting ties with: Dan Gilroy's Breakfast Club! Now Madonna and Bray parted company completely.

But that was not the whole of Madonna's ordeal. She now had to tell Kamins that he would not be used either. When she told him, he reacted.

"Sure, I was hurt," he said. "I felt stepped on, because it was always understood that I would produce her, but later I realized she was making the right career move."

Actually Madonna had given Kamins's own career a big boost. "Madonna manipulates her own way, but I don't think there's a mean bone in her body," Kamins said later. "Well, maybe a knuckle or two."

The fact that Madonna had been forced to break with two of her best friends left her with a bereft, lost feeling, but she was too professional to brood over it for long.

"I felt guilty because I felt like I was traveling through people. But I think that's true of most ambitious, driven people. You take what you can [get], then [you] move on. If the people can't move with you—whether it's a physical or emotional move—I feel sad about that. That's part of the tragedy of love." Love, or success.

The producer who was eventually selected by the Warner Bros. top brass—with Madonna's approval—to make her debut album was Reggie Lucas. Lucas had won his spurs working with such fine female vocalists as Stephanie Mills and Roberta Flack. And Lucas in turn hired a skilled group of sidemen to make the cuts: people who had backed up obvious stars, such as Aretha Franklin.

But Lucas had other talents as well. It was he who wrote "Borderline," one of the songs that would be featured on the initial Madonna album.

While "Everybody" was, according to all indications, doing well in the United States, it was lagging behind substantially in England and abroad. The money men at Warners decided that Madonna could use some exposure in London, and while there, she might help boost the slow sales of her single.

She was booked into the top London clubs, with opening night at the Camden Palace. Of the dozens of celebrities invited, less than half the list of freebies even bothered to attend the opening show. Her other appearances were less than auspicious. She did the best she could to try to arouse interest in her act, but sales continued to lag.

When she returned to the States, she found that things were even more negative there. In fact everything was at a total impasse. Nothing had happened while she was away. She called in her friend Benitez to act as her adviser on the material that would be used in the projected album.

Once Madonna was on the scene again, things began to move. Benitez's help was needed, and the results of his work were excellent. One by one the cuts were made, with Lucas giving his all to working out the unlucky "Ain't No Big Deal," the song that was once again planned as the flagship of Madonna's fleet.

And yet, and yet—

"Unbelievable," Rosenblatt recalled, "the song, yet again, didn't work out. The supposed lead song of the album was simply unusable."

The brass huddled and studied the cuts, listening to them over and over again. There was nothing for it but to kill "Ain't No Big Deal" again. Even if it *was* to be the star of the lineup, it simply was not working out right. And again the killing of "No Big Deal" was a serious setback. The album, which was originally titled *Lucky Star*—from one of the songs featured—

was suddenly way over budget, largely because of the fiasco of "Ain't No Big Deal"—and was now lacking a key song.

Rosenblatt had an idea.

He would use Madonna in a tough confrontation with top management. To employ the football term, Madonna would carry the ball on this play. She would fly out *with* him to Los Angeles to sweet-talk the Warner Bros. brass into advancing some cash to replace the ailing song.

In the end Rosenblatt's strategy proved successful. He explained, "She was so warm and bubbly, so much fun, that everybody out there loved her. This accomplished, I explained that 'Ain't No Big Deal' had to be replaced on the album. They gave us more money. And we went back to the studio to record another song."

The "other song"—?

It was Jellybean Benitez who had been carrying around a demo tape of a disco song written by a pair of writers named Curtis Hudson and Lisa Stevens. The song was titled "Holiday." Madonna had heard it and liked it.

So, it was Madonna, who had final approval, who suggested the replacement for "Ain't No Big Deal." It would be "Holiday." And to make it, she and Benitez once again teamed up, working closely together and giving it everything they had.

"He turned into my producer and my boyfriend," Madonna said, speaking of Benitez. "Everything happened at the same time. We were both very ambitious and we both wanted to be stars." This could be their breakthrough.

There was sufficient chemistry between the two performers to make "Holiday" a special song—and indeed it did turn out to be the top song of the album. Selected as the leadoff single to introduce the album, "Holiday" was released in June 1983, with very high hopes.

Those high hopes were to be dashed almost immediately. "Holiday" performed sluggishly in the charts and was only a modest success after its release in the summer. This did not augur too well for the upcoming release of the album in which it was supposedly the big number. It was depressing to Madonna to realize that what she had thought would be a big hit as an ordinary single was barely limping along.

While her professional life seemed to be slowing up, her personal life was improving considerably. She and Benitez had moved into a warehouse loft in the now-fashionable SoHo section of Manhattan.

"It was huge—two thousand square feet at least—with wooden floors and windows on every wall," Madonna recalled. "We had a bed, a table overlooking the street, and lots of mirrors for my choreography. All the artists lived there. David Byrne from Talking Heads was a neighbor."

Madonna and Benitez hit it off very well now. After all, they were more or less launching their careers together. They both seemed to be taking off at the same time. And yet Madonna was beginning to have second thoughts. Was a touch of that "killjoy" character flaw she had inherited from her hard-nosed father suddenly reappearing in her makeup?

She was worried about the album's musical approach. Wasn't it just a bit too smooth and slick for the real Madonna?

"I wanted a sound that was mine," she said later, "and it wasn't until the album was nearly finished that I thought, 'Hey, I know a lot more about this than I'm giving myself credit for.' "

Actually Madonna thought Reggie Lucas's efforts were just a bit overdone for her own special taste. She felt that a sparser, thinner sound would have been better. However, she had put herself in the hands of the top brass at Warner Bros.—and as far as she was concerned, what they said still went.

However, with second thoughts creeping in on her and keeping her awake at night sometimes, she decided that it would not be Reggie Lucas who made her second album—if she were lucky enough to *get* a second album. What she needed from somebody was more astute leadership. What she needed was not a producer. What she needed was a manager.

Her thoughts led her to a way out of the trap she had constructed for herself. Who was the singer whom she preferred above all others? Michael Jackson.

"[Michael Jackson] transcended almost every level and appealed to everyone, and he had conquered the world," Madonna thought. "I want *his* manager."

Who *was* Michael Jackson's manager? Freddie DeMann.

Now, in the midst of the doldrums of summer, and in the face of sagging sales for "Holiday," both in the States and in Britain, Madonna took a jetliner out to Los Angeles to look up Freddie DeMann.

Somehow she talked her way into the guarded portals that kept the world away from the sacred precincts of Freddie DeMann's sanctum sanctorum. Eventually she charmed Freddie DeMann himself. He was impressed.

"She had that special magic that very few stars have," he said of Madonna later. He promised her that he would come to New York to see her act.

He did exactly that. On his next rip to New York he took in her act at Studio 54, not realizing that Madonna was suffering from nerves and everything else at the time he watched her. In spite of her misgivings and her fears that DeMann would think her less than a star, the manager liked the show and came in to talk to her.

Later DeMann opined, "She will be a female Michael Jackson."

The important conversation between the two of them was all business. He agreed to become her manager. It was a coup d'état for Madonna.

Viewing her in retrospect some eight years later DeMann told a slightly different version of the story of their meeting.

"Madonna is more sophisticated [now in 1991] than she was eight years ago, but she has the same sensibilities as she had on the first day I met her. She had balls then and she has them now. I remember when she first walked into my office . . .

"She had three problems that day, three pressing problems, and I said, 'I'll make three calls and take care of your problems.' And I did it. The next day she called with five problems. The next day she had eight. The next day ten. I said, 'How can one person have all these problems?' She said, 'Well, I do.' Madonna has that ability to grab you by the lapels, and soon all you can think about is her."

Madonna's album, retitled *Madonna* and released as such, was in the meantime making its way sluggishly onto the charts. "Holiday," the single produced to ignite a great fire to cause the album to incandesce on first appearance, lay languid in the summer heat. In Britain the *Madonna* album was dead in the water. The singles, "Holiday" and "Lucky Star," were just as inert.

But those weren't the only two songs on the album. Madonna still had great faith in "Everybody." Yet "Everybody" was dying on the vine too.

She knew the record was good, and one of these days Warner Bros. and the rest of them were going to figure it out.

But when would that be?

In order not to let the grass grow under her feet, Madonna worked up a dance number to play against "Everybody" in the style of an MTV video. When she had it worked out, she called Rosenblatt and asked him if he could help her get it produced as a short dance video. Rosenblatt picked up the phone and dialed a man named Ed Steinberg, who was the video producer and founder of Rock America. That was the company responsible for mass distribution of rock videos to disco clubs all over the country.

For the uninitiated: A dance video is *not* an MTV, but is a cousin to MTV. Steinberg knew all the ins and outs of the business and found that he could work well with Madonna. In a few days Madonna had her three dancers ready, and Steinberg brought in the film crew to start shooting.

"Madonna is incredibly cool under pressure," Steinberg recalled. "The day I shot 'Everybody,' one of her three backup dancers didn't show up, which would have cracked most people under the circumstances."

Did Madonna crumble under the stress? Absolutely not.

"Madonna stayed in complete control," Steinberg said. "Very patiently and very efficiently she rechoreographed the entire song, following all of my directions for what would and wouldn't work on video. Madonna is hot in video for the simple reason that she is a class act."

He had more to say about her.

"Working with Madonna is like working with Michael Jackson. She's a uniquely talented performer who can dance, sing, and act incredibly well. She's a director's dream because all one needs to do to get a great video is to faithfully record her performance rather than, as with many acts, rely on audiovisual trickery."

Something happened in the middle of summer that could have been scripted by a Hollywood film hack. Somehow "Holiday" began to take on a life of its own and started coming up in the charts. By the end of the year the single had turned into a miraculous member of the Top Twenty Christmas Hits. It was being played everywhere!

Madonna had not been home to Michigan to see her family for two years. At Thanksgiving, with the hit single "Holiday" doing so well, she returned to her hometown and brought Jellybean Benitez with her.

"The last time I'd been home," Madonna said, "I was starving, and they all went, 'You are disgusting.' But now they'd heard my record on the radio, and I figured my father would finally be convinced that going to the University of Michigan was not the only alternative for me."

Was Silvio Ciccone convinced? Well, almost.

"He was quite proud of me, although he didn't approve of it *all*."

He *did* approve of Madonna's debut album. How could he not? On the jacket it was dedicated to Silvio Ciccone.

8

VISION QUEST

In spite of all the excitement she was creating in the entertainment industry, Madonna had not yet earned one split second of time on the magic eye of television, the god of all singers, dancers, and entertainers—in the favored spot of MTV.

When Madonna had finished her dance video of "Holiday," Rosenblatt conceded that although it was a good tape, it did not quite have the potential for the very special field of MTV.

"We just figured we couldn't do it with 'Holiday,' " he said, "because it was too dance-oriented for the MTV format. The way an artist gets airplay on MTV is when a major record company, such as Warner Brothers, goes to bat for the artist, demonstrating that they are solidly behind the act."

But Rosenblatt had something up his sleeve. He thought he knew what *might* work for MTV. It was a production of "Burning Up," one of the numbers in the *Madonna* album.

It was a Madonna-inspired piece all the way. She had written it herself. It was blatantly sexual, the idea expressed in the title as well as in the words. The singer is "burning up" with desire, frustrated by this and that, and finally breaks through in the end in a flaming climax.

It was the structure of the song that intrigued Rosenblatt. It was as effective dramatically as it was lyrically. With one submissive sexual innuendo after another, the song finally reaches its climax with the singer admitting that she has no shame, that she is not like other women, that she will do anything she wants to, that she has no regard for the consequences of her actions, that she is, above all, her own person.

When it finally came to writing and casting the filmic action scenes to underscore the song's lyrics, Kenny Compton, one of Madonna's off-and-on boyfriends, was cast in the part of a truck driver who was trying to run her down on the highway.

It was just after the production was wrapped that he came in to see his one-time lover and told her, quite unambiguously, that their relationship, which had lasted for over two years, was over and that he would never be seeing her again.

Madonna was stunned. "It was the longest monogamous relationship I'd had at the time," she admitted later a bit ruefully. She meant "monogamous" on her part, not particularly on his. And she meant "monogamous" before the advent of Jellybean Benitez.

It was not just the idea of MTV that got Madonna thinking on a bigger scale—that is, on the scale of the big silver screen. She had always been thinking eventually of motion pictures. But with that earlier shot of acting in *A Certain Sacrifice* and with the two videos she had now made, she decided that she would broaden herself just a bit for the future. Records were one thing; performing at discos was another; the big time was in film. And the money.

So she signed up to study acting with Mira Rostova. Rostova was high on Method acting—the kind of thing Stanislavsky had brought to fame and the style of acting that had made Marlon Brando the big superstar he was.

"Music was still very important to me," Madonna said, "but I had always had a great interest in films, and the thought that I could only make records for the rest of my life filled me with horror."

Many earlier stars had developed into singers, and many earlier singers had developed into stars. The two careers frequently went hand in glove. Doris Day, for example, had been a singer who had developed into a fine comedic actress.

"I didn't see it as being so diverse," she argued. "After you've done an album, you often have to wait around for six months while it's promoted, so I thought I might as well act in that time." Or at least take *lessons*.

Madonna finally signed on with the William Morris Agency and was called in to audition for a number of pictures. One of these was a projected film titled *Footloose*. This was a story about a streetwise dancer who moves to a small town where dancing is outlawed by a hellfire-and-brimstone preacher. The conflict between the minister and the dancer is the centerpiece of the plot.

Madonna was turned down for the role.

Another film was *Vision Quest*. Madonna once reported on it in this way:

"It was a coming-of-age movie about a guy who's training for the Olympics. In the end he wins his big fight, but loses his girl."

Madonna was offered a small part as a nightclub singer. She did three songs for the soundtrack of the motion picture, which was scored by Phil Ramone, he of the exciting *Flashdance*.

"It wasn't exactly an acting role, but it was a bona fide movie, and it was an invaluable foot in the door," Madonna said later.

When the film was released, two of the songs she made for the soundtrack were used: "Crazy for You" and "The Gambler." In England the film was rereleased later under the new title of *Crazy for You*!

One brief description of the film called it "muddled," "overlong," with "too many familiar elements." It mentions Madonna's performance singing "Crazy for You."

Meanwhile "Burning Up" was perking along on MTV, and with the door now opened up, Madonna worked on another MTV of a song from her album "Borderline."

"Borderline" found her playing a more or less familiar role. She is a good-time girl who hangs out on Manhattan's Lower West Side. She runs with a spray-paint gang—a rough and streetwise young chick with a soft and sensitive center. She is a graffiti queen wrapped up in a sexpot package.

The reaction to her role in this MTV was very positive. Young fans thought that she was very cool and contained. Soon she was being hailed as the sexiest blonde now singing. Was she another Marilyn Monroe? Hard to tell.

"I feel slightly entertained when people say I'm a sex symbol," Madonna said. "I don't take it seriously, but I think that if you evoke sexuality through music, it's natural."

After "Borderline" she made "Lucky Star," another number from the same album. This was in February 1984, and the album was still on the charts. Madonna was now solidly established in the MTV world with three productions; her album was selling well over the hundred thousand mark that Rosenblatt had only dreamed of; she had made it all on low-budget productions and on her own talent.

In the entertainment business most successes are achieved with at least two elements of promotion that Madonna did not have: a big band to back her up and a live tour that would put her in front of hundreds of thousands of paying fans.

Even though Madonna's strongest feature was her ability to perform live in front of an audience, she had only appeared in a few "guest" performances in small American and European clubs. At that most of her "performances" were simply lip-synch pantomimes.

Her videotapes served as substitutes for the two important elements lacking in her buildup. They cut down on the phenomenally high expense of maintaining a backup band; salaries, costumes, hotels, meals, transportation, equipment, rehearsals, and so on. She did it without that expense, thanks to the potency of video.

"I think video has been very important to my success," she said. "There's a lot more risk involved in live performance than video, because there are so many things that can go wrong."

By the time the MTV "Lucky Star" was made and released in 1984, Rosenblatt was in ecstasy. "That single," he said, referring to "Lucky Star," "sent album sales through the roof. I mean, how many hits were on that album?"

Actually there were six—six Top Ten dance hits on one

album! Of the eight songs on the album, only two tunes were not released as singles. The other six—the hits—were "Everybody," "I Know It," "Lucky Star," "Holiday," "Think of Me," and "Borderline."

Warner Bros. sent her to London again early in the year to try to stir up some excitement about "Holiday," which had never really gone anywhere since the end of 1983. Madonna was subjected to an endless series of interviews by the press, and as a result of this tremendous media blitz, the single finally moved up into the Top Sixty.

She worked hard, appearing on *The Tube* and *Top of the Pops* on television, and managed to nudge the single finally up to Number Six—a long way from Number Sixty! To the British her tongue-in-cheek dance routines were rather appealing. Actually the British sense of humor caught on to her putdown of the material and helped rather than hindered her public image.

"People seeing me for the first time must have thought I was a fruitcake," she told the Fleet Street gang, "a real live wire, but I can't come on and be sexy without humor." She missed the point; the British understood her probably better than the Americans.

In fact the record-buying public was amused at Madonna's getup: from her streetwise insouciance, her flauntedly visible belly button, her midriff tops, net skirts, thick socks, crucifix earrings, and enormous rubber bracelets. She had brass, and her whole image was that of a cheeky woman who had the guts to challenge the traditional rock territory then in the grip of pelvis-shaking rock-and-role singers.

Her costume and the way she wore it made a definite statement. Her overall look was trampy and punk. Her music was for dancing, and her vocal sound was girlish in the extreme. Her songs were upbeat, and each oozed sex. She wore the bracelets and crucifixes to enhance her tramp and punk image.

For some reason she misread the English public. She felt that they were annoyed at her aggressive New York style, since it was so distinctly at odds with the tradition of the British stiff upper lip as a means of confronting misfortune or adversity. She felt ill at ease in England.

"I like England, but it isn't what I'm used to," she told a British journalist. "In New York, people are loud and say what they think; in London you're so reserved. When I laugh out loud in the streets here, everyone stares, and I feel like I'm doing something wrong. On the tube no one speaks or smiles— in New York they assault you with noise."

In spite of her hard-won and newfound success, she told them, "Most times people aren't very nice to me here in England."

And that didn't help her image any. Again she missed the point. It wouldn't be until the next time around that she would begin to find out the truth.

Back home in New York Madonna found herself itching to get back to work, to write some fresh material, to transform what she needed to transform in her image, to go with her strengths and overcome her weaknesses.

She was thinking that her second album would be "harder and aggressive with stronger songs."

She still had loyalty to her beginnings. No matter what she did, she would never lose touch with her street background. Even if she wanted to get out of the gutter, she knew where she had been, and she would always revel in the memory of it.

"I had the same friends," she told a writer. "I went to the same divey restaurants in the East Village, and I rode the subway every day because I wasn't that noticeable, although I had a lot of young girl fans who'd start squealing on the trains and asking me if I was *really* Madonna."

And so Madonna finally got back to work and found herself rushing ahead like a house afire on her second album. With the help of her new manager, Freddie DeMann, she zeroed in on Nile Rodgers, the producer who had helped make such a big hit of David Bowie.

Good-bye, Steve Bray; so long, Mark Kamins; hello, Nile Rodgers.

The chemistry between Rodgers and Madonna was excellent. He agreed with her that she should get away from the rather slick and smooth sound of the first album and do something more elemental, more solid, more funky.

"Nile's a passionate man, who lives life to the hilt," Madonna said of her producer. "He's a genius. I had a lot more confidence in myself and a lot more to do with the way the album came out soundwise. I worked side by side with Nile, and he was very open with me."

By now Madonna knew she had to speak up about what she really wanted. And she did. Rodgers was quite frank about her. "She was more temperamental than anyone else I'd ever worked with, but with her it's not a bad thing. When she throws a tantrum, it's because something's really bothering her. She's just fantastic."

As the new order changed, so did the personnel around Madonna, as it had always done when a certain Rubicon had been crossed.

Jellybean Benitez, who had figured so prominently in the first album, did not figure quite so prominently in the second.

"He's got his own work and he's a technician rather than a musician," Madonna explained. And that seemed to be about it for Benitez. He had come into her life when she was on the verge of a big breakthrough. He had worked with her and helped her. In doing so, he had also helped himself. When Madonna's second album came through, he was more or less in the past tense.

Oddly enough, Madonna returned to an earlier boyfriend, associate, and good companion.

"I need someone to help me with some songs," Madonna told Steve Bray. And he climbed aboard the Madonna bandwagon again. This time to cowrite four songs with Madonna. Of course Bray had been miffed at being betrayed by her, but somehow he found it easy to forgive, forget, and bury the assaults on his pride.

"The relationship was too old to have something like that stand in its way," he observed suavely.

The lead song of the second album was called "Like a Virgin," which would also be the title of the album. Together Rodgers and Madonna plotted out the background for a video that would give the romantic, mysterious background to the lyrics. The place to film was finally selected as Venice, Italy.

Warner Bros. sent the group abroad to film the video on

location; it would be released separately from the album. The scenes would be shot in and around Venice—an excellent setting, certainly. However, there was one memorable character in the scenario that was a surprise to Madonna.

To add exotic surrealism and mystery and eroticism, Rodgers chose to bring in a real live, "tame" lion. Madonna did not relish the scene she had to film with the lion, even though it became the most interesting part of the final MTV.

"The lion didn't do anything he was supposed to do," Madonna complained. "I ended up leaning against this pillar with his head in my crotch."

She shivered at the recollection of the scene. She knew that she felt sure the lion was going to try to take a bite out of her. She even lifted the veil she was wearing to try to stare the beast down.

"He opened his mouth and let out this huge roar. I got so frightened my heart fell into my shoes. When he finally walked away, the director yelled, 'Cut,' and I had to take a long breather. But I could really *relate* to the lion. I felt like in a past life I was a lion or a cat or something."

With that, Madonna returned to New York to get back to work. "Like a Virgin" was being talked about, and she was asked for a prerelease performance of the new song at the MTV Video Awards ceremony at Radio City.

The video, shown there, went down very well with the crowd, and as Madonna walked back to her limo at the end of the show, she saw a huge crowd of young fans filling the street and cheering for her as she tried to slip into the waiting car.

Maripol, Madonna's designer friend, was with her at the time. She was surprised at Madonna's bewildered response to all this adulation.

"She was looking at all the kids and she was wondering what she was doing sitting there in the limo. She wanted to be there, with them, in the street, yelling at herself. I looked at her face. It was pure innocence and pure joy."

Madonna failed to see that in the same way she wanted to be out there with them, they wanted to be sitting in the limo in her place! Nor did she notice another interesting thing.

Those fans were beginning to *look like her*! They wanted to *be* her!

Things were beginning to change dramatically in the world of Madonna. Her tastes and values were going through a rapid metamorphosis. She had decided that hard work was the best thing to keep her happy. And the keystone of hard work was good health. In order to do her best work and keep in good health, she decided that the New York night scene was not the best thing for her.

She wanted to "keep a low profile and see the sun shine, take care of myself, and get enough sleep, because I had to look healthy on camera."

Jellybean Benitez still lived for the noisy nightlife of the Funhouse. Madonna opted for another life-style.

"She became obsessed with keeping her body in shape," Benitez complained. "But people didn't realize how incredibly intelligent she was. She loved reading English literature: Shakespeare and Keats. She'd spend hours plowing through their works."

Meanwhile the second album was taking shape and would be released in September 1984.

Madonna in the 1985 film *Desperately Seeking Susan*, the role that showed everyone she was more than just a pop star.

Madonna performing at the Live Aid concert shortly after the scandal about her posing for nude photographs made headlines

Madonna, looking anything but the glamorous star, is caught by a paparazzo after one of her daily workouts.

During the filming of the towering flop *Shanghai Surprise*, which co-starred her then-husband, Sean Penn, Madonna was hounded by the British press at every turn. Here she is caught leaving a London restaurant with her brother, Christopher Ciccone.

To this day, Madonna says that Sean has been the one great love in her life.

The King of Late Night meets the Queen of Hype: Johnny Carson greets Madonna on a 1987 appearance on the *Tonight* show.

On her jogs, Madonna is always accompanied by bodyguards and a handful of in-shape photographers.

Madonna braves the crush of reporters at the 1987 post-premiere party for *Who's That Girl?*, her second bomb in a row after *Shanghai Surprise*.

9

DESPERATELY SEEKING FAME

In 1982 an enterprising young film director named Susan Seidelman had created a minor sensation in the industry by bringing in a low-budget film titled *Smithereens* and turning it into a surefire hit. Even in 1982 the sum of eighty thousand dollars was a pittance to spend on the production of a motion picture. More so for a film that garnered critical success as well as money at the box office.

The story of *Smithereens* concerned the adventures of an East Village hustler named Wren, played by Susan Berman, and her attempts at making her dreams of success as a punk rock band manager come true. Probably the most memorable sequence in the film was one involving Berman and a chicken salad sandwich. "Solid characterization and simple, fluid direction" was the assessment of Leonard Maltin in the 1990 edition of *TV Movies and Video Guide*.

Seidelman was looking around for a second film venture and found it in an expertly crafted screenplay by Leora Barish titled *Desperately Seeking Susan*. In a point of fact "Susan" is not the main character, but a foil to the protagonist. The main character is Roberta, a bored housewife from New Jersey married to a boring jacuzzi salesman. Rosanna Arquette was immediately cast as the lead, Roberta, with the role of Susan open for tryouts.

The casting was tricky. Susan, an energetic, free-living East Village soul, who sleeps around for convenience as much as pleasure, must not appear to be a hopeless slut or even a sophisticated woman playing at being a bimbo for kicks. She had to be *real*.

Also, Susan must be an opposite number to Roberta, without slipping over into parody or satire. That is, everything that the staid Roberta is, Susan is *not*. Over two hundred people thought they had a handle on the role and tried out for the part.

Eventually it was Seidelman herself who approached Madonna to play the role of Susan. She had seen her on MTV and had listened to her records. Madonna's new agent had presented Madonna with a script of the film before the meeting. She immediately sized up the character of Susan as eerily similar to her own "wild, free-spirited, and adventurous" nature.

In fact it was the life-style of the Susan character that rather faithfully mirrored Madonna's early days as a self-styled hustler on the streets of New York, just "living off the kindness of strangers."

Leora Barish, the script writer, might have written the story with Madonna in mind, although she had not even heard of her when she was putting the story together.

At the first meeting between Seidelman and Madonna, Madonna simply played herself as much as she could. She thought that in that manner she could invest the character with everything the role seemed to need.

"She was nervous and vulnerable and not at all arrogant," Seidelman said later. "Sweet, but intelligent and verbal, with a sense of humor. I just started seeing her as Susan."

By the time Madonna had auditioned with the other two hundred hopefuls, she knew that she had the best chance in the world simply because Madonna *was* Susan.

She was only partially right. Seidelman selected Madonna for the role not because she *was* Susan, but because of the "natural screen presence" she thought Madonna definitely had.

"She has a kind of face you want to look at blown up fifty feet," Seidelman said later. "She isn't conventionally beautiful, but then neither were Bette Davis or Marlene Dietrich. I didn't choose her because she was a rock star. I'm interested in interesting people."

When Seidelman signed her up to play Susan, Madonna was only an up-and-coming pop star, with one slow-moving album out, and a lot of potential somewhere in the wings. However, by the time the shooting began in New York in November 1984, her own status had changed in a dramatic and stunning fashion.

The album *Like a Virgin* had been taped, edited, and readied to go in July 1984, but the lethargic and sluggish performance of the first album had suddenly been transformed into an exciting and memorable upward trend in the charts. Because of *Madonna*'s abrupt reincarnation, Warner Bros. postponed the release of *Like a Virgin* so that it would not compete with *Madonna*'s second life. Ironically the second album was finally released in November 1984, at the very moment the real Madonna was in front of the camera as Susan.

The second album did not follow the pattern of the first. In fact it exploded instantly to become an almost overnight hit. With Madonna's first album a growing success, and her second a supersuccess, Madonna found herself on the way to becoming a kind of megastar.

Success does not always breed love and affection. What happened on the set of *Desperately Seeking Susan* was not pretty. In a turnaround, Madonna seemed to be getting all the good press. She was becoming very big in a field allied to film; and that made her presence in the film more and more important.

It was apparent to Rosanna Arquette, starred in the film and certainly top banana, that Madonna was getting all the attention from the media and she was getting hardly any at all. And the media, sensitive to nuances and subtleties in personality, picked up on her snappishness and suddenly made her—Arquette—the spokesperson for the film.

"I thought I was going to be making this small, charming film—not some rock video," Arquette snapped to those who would listen. They loved the sound of her words and printed the statement everywhere. Then they began picking up on Arquette and comparing her to Madonna. Their backgrounds were, amazingly, somewhat similar.

Arquette had left home at the age of seventeen—just like Madonna—and sought her own fortune by traveling all the way across the country to Hollywood. She had of course hitchhiked her way, and that in itself was an interesting character element, the kind of detail the press lapped up.

But Arquette's problem was that she had paid her dues as an up-and-coming actress. She had worked hard making it in Hollywood. Why should she be playing second banana to a video personality who had come in through the side door?

Kinky little disagreements and digs at one another surfaced constantly during the filming of the picture. Seidelman continued to try to pour soothing syrup over the troubled waters, but with little success.

To the press Seidelman expressed the opinion that the two women stars resembled "the two most popular cheerleaders in school—on the surface they were really friendly, but underneath they couldn't wait to poke fun at each other."

Interestingly enough, Seidelman had unwittingly characterized Madonna as exactly what Madonna was in her high school years—a fledgling cheerleader!

Seidelman had her troubles with Madonna, but she had them with Arquette as well. There were occasional conflicts of an artistic nature that led the two actresses to storm at one another and fling abuse about in quick-tempered onslaughts.

When the vibrations got out of hand and the atmosphere was thick enough to cut, Madonna would wander about shaking her head. Mark Blum, who played Arquette's husband in the picture, found a good way to bring Madonna back to earth.

"He'd tell me a joke and chill me out," Madonna recalled.

But there was more fuel for the fire in the offing. Madonna had been cast in the role of Susan simply as a free-wheeling Village hustler—*not* a singer. During the rehearsals of scenes in nightclubs and other East Village dives, Madonna had provided one of her demo tapes for background music, simply to substitute for the real musicians who would come in later and dub for the master.

Seidelman was attracted to one track that Madonna had cut. It was a song called "Into the Groove." It existed only in demo form, not having been recorded professionally yet. Seidelman became aware that the song might have good commercial potential—for the picture itself.

It was Seidelman's decision eventually to incorporate the song into the soundtrack. In fact its selection for use in the picture was a definite compliment to Madonna. It made the casting of Madonna more important than it would have been had she performed simply as an actress.

Unfortunately Madonna did not see it exactly that way. She thought it was "a drag, because I was trying to establish myself as an actress, not as a singer making movies."

Madonna had more to say—particularly about filmmaking in general. She claimed that making a film was a "drag" and went on to say, "There was so much sitting around, it drove me crazy, but it's what I'd always wanted to do."

She discovered something else. When she got her first call to set up before the cameras, she found that she was a victim of double-digit stage fright. Even with all her prior training in the videos and all her years on the stage behind her, she froze on-camera and was sometimes unable to utter a syllable.

"I had a few scenes where I was really shitting bricks!" she said, a typical Madonna observation. "A few times I was so nervous, I opened my mouth and nothing came out. I think I surprised everybody, though, by being one of the calmest people on the set, because I was in total wonderment, just soaking everything up."

The discipline demanded on the set did not bother her at all. She had always prided herself on being in total self-control.

"At first it was hard to get producers to take me seriously because I was a rock star," she said once. "I guess they thought I would throw fits or do blow [cocaine] on the set or something. I think they were shocked when I showed up every morning like clockwork."

Seidelman was impressed by Madonna's dedication. "She is an incredibly disciplined person. During the shoot we would

often go home at eleven or twelve at night and have to be
back on the set by six or seven the next morning. Half that
time the driver would pick up Madonna at her health club.
She'd get up at four-thirty in the morning to work out first."

Throughout the nine weeks of shooting, Madonna was
required to consume vast amounts of cheese puffs. She knew
that cheese was extremely fattening. In order to try to cut down
on overeating, she would spit out the puffs at the end of each
scene. And her workouts every morning tended to keep her
fit. Madonna, incidentally, had always suffered from insom-
nia and usually needed only a few hours of sleep each night.

As filming progressed, Madonna found herself becoming
more and more identified with the character she was playing.
Susan, she found, reminded her more and more of Madonna.

"She's this really crazy, lively, wild girl who kind of wreaks
havoc in everyone's life. I can relate to that. She drifts in and
out of guys' lives and they fall in love with her and she says
'later' and stuff like that. The difference is she is kind of a
drifter and I am very focused."

As she watched the rushes, Madonna began to believe in
the picture, and, indeed, in herself as well. It was, in her words,
a "screwball mystery movie" about "mistaken identities, stolen
earrings, and Egyptian symbolism." She saw it as a reprise of
a Golden Age movie. "It was like a return to the simple caper
comedies Claudette Colbert and Carole Lombard made in the
thirties. They gave you a taste of real life, some poignance,
and left you feeling up at the end."

In spite of the conflict on the set between Arquette and
Madonna—and even between Seidelman and her two stars—
the picture was finished on schedule and turned out on
screening to be one of the better pictures of the year.

Vincent Canby was enthusiastic in *The New York Times*.
He called Madonna "one of the hottest personalities in music
video" and said that she had played her first major role in a
theatrical film and carried it off with "nervy ease."

One of the major elements in the success of Madonna's
conception of the role was the quirky wardrobe in which she
appeared—not really very different from Madonna's original
costume on the cover of her first album. "Miniskirts, rhine-

stone boots, and New Wave junk—performance art on the hoof," Canby called it.

What intrigued most of the film audience was the interesting exchange of personalities involved in the quick-witted script. The main gimmick of the story is the sudden crossover between Susan, the Village hustler, and Roberta, the square suburbanite. Arquette finds herself enjoying the sybaritic and aimless life of the hustler, and Madonna finds herself enjoying the straitlaced, boring life of a suburban spouse.

"Miss Arquette and Madonna are delights," Canby wrote, "as is each member of the huge supporting cast." "Madonna, the pretty, punkish, eerily unexcitable music-video performer," and Susan, "an especially aimless, vaguely New Wave, East Village character who finds herself mixed up in a gangland murder."

The film, Canby noted, "somehow succeeds in being both fast-paced and almost leisurely. It's sharp but unaggressively hip in a manner that is absolutely contemporary and, though [Seidelman is] certainly aware of films past, [the film] doesn't require that the audience share that awareness or understand what she's up to."

Madonna, Canby said, is "as pungent a presence on the big screen as on the small one." High praise indeed.

Canby's rave was not the only one. Most of the reviewing fraternity operated on the same wavelength. The only person involved who, surprisingly, did not seem to share the feelings of the critics was Madonna herself.

She simply did not understand what all the fuss was about. She had done a job the best she could—and here everyone was claiming her a genius of some kind!

"I had no idea it would be a hit," she said about the film. "I think it worked because it's a comedy that defies description. It's not pratfalls, like so many teenage films, and it's not a cult art film, like *Down by Law*. It's somewhere in between."

When Madonna finally saw *Desperately Seeking Susan*, she realized that it was probably better than she had imagined it to be when she was working on it.

"My favorite scene in the movie is when I'm in the straight guy's apartment. It's a complete mess; I've eaten all the food, and we're in bed smoking a joint. I don't have any method of acting, but I just knew that scene was funny."

Reminded that the scene more or less condoned the smoking of marijuana and that it might make some of her fans and their parents nervous, Madonna laughed.

"I didn't write the script. It's just a role. She's rebellious, and kids relate to that and always have."

As for *her* feelings about films and the roles she should play: "I don't condone violence," she told movie critic Gene Siskel, "and I don't believe I would ever play a victimized character, unless it was properly resolved by the end of the film. With hard drugs the same would have to be true."

Desperately Seeking Susan did not open until March 1985. By then Madonna's second album, *Like a Virgin,* had entered the charts at Number Seventy and had skyrocketed almost instantly up to the Number One spot in the New Year of 1985. Her "Virgin" single was also in the Number One spot. This certainly bolstered her image as a singing star—the image that her role in the film imaginatively portrayed.

Nevertheless there were problems.

The purists in the real world were worried about the conflicted imagery of Madonna's "virginity"—as proclaimed by the title of the album and lead song—and her image as a voluptuous, sexy, and blushing bride on the cover of the album.

The working press, which had supported her previously, turned on her. Kurt Loder, in *Rolling Stone,* charged her with being a flesh peddler.

"Madonna's bare-bellied, fondle-my-bra image," he wrote, seemed to be more an admission of "sex sells" than any kind of proof of singing and performing talent.

Michael Rosenblatt immediately came to her defense. "I find it ridiculous when people accuse Madonna of selling sex. Sex and rock and roll fit together so perfectly that everyone in this business sells sex. Boy George, the Beatles, Elvis Presley, Van Halen, Prince—who isn't selling sex? Maybe Barry Manilow, but that's only because he's after an older market, so he sells love."

Rosenblatt went on. "Madonna isn't pushing sex anything like she could if she really wanted to. Her look is a hot

'I'm a one-hundred-percent woman' look, and I think that's great. Rock is full of boys who look like girls and girls who look like boys. Madonna doesn't have to put on black leather and kick the shit out of a motorcycle gang to be cool. I don't understand why people find a girl looking like a girl to be at all offensive. She's not a stripper type, so what's the problem?''

Madonna defended herself. "I don't think I'm using sex to sell myself. I'm a very sexual person, and that comes through in my music."

The controversy caused Rosenblatt to elaborate a bit about the state of the singing and performing arts. "Music has gotten very demanding on the young performing artist," he said. "Imagine a field that asks a young person to master the complex technical and artistic problems of making a record, then expects them to be an actor too! Yet Madonna masters it all so quickly, so easily, and will increase her audience exponentially with movies, reaching people who might not hear her music.

"I sort of hate to say this, but Madonna could almost become—wow! I can't *believe* I would say this—but she can become big like Barbra Streisand; a first-rate singer and a box-office draw in the movies: Madonna can be massive in both worlds."

In order to cool off a bit the public perception of Madonna as "selling sex," she was asked to explain the video story accompanying the lead song in her second album, "Like a Virgin."

About the location of the story in Venice, Madonna pointed out that that city was always traditionally known as the city of love. She had come prepared and threw in a little history and literature. In fact, she said, Venice was the home of the world's most renowned lover, Casanova.

"We wanted me to be the modern-day, worldly wise girl that I am," Madonna said. "But then we wanted to go back in time and use an ancient virgin [for contrast]."

Madonna pointed out that the action of the video moves back and forth between two separate versions of Madonna—one a woman in a nearly sacred long white dress and the other a bare-bellied, gyrating sexpot. Madonna at one point chases a man whose face is hidden in a carnival mask; in all, the effect is a dreamlike sequence of sex and romance.

With the historical background and the literary significance of the setting in Venice established, Madonna then pointed out how she felt when some people were turned off by her performance.

"I was surprised with how people reacted to 'Like a Virgin,' because when I did the song, to me, I was singing about how something made me feel a certain way—brand-new and fresh—and everyone else interpreted it as 'I don't want to be a virgin anymore. Fuck my brains out.' That's not what I sang at all."

As for the rosary wrapped around her neck and the crucifixes hanging from her ears—surely this was blatant sacrilege deliberately intended to shock?

"With the crucifixes I was exorcising the extremes that my upbringing dwelt on. Putting them up on the wall and throwing darts at them."

What about the BOY TOY belt slung under her bare navel?

"And the BOY TOY thing was a joke—a tag name given to me when I first arrived in New York because I flirted with the boys. All the graffiti artists wore their nicknames on their belt buckles."

She confessed that at times she had cast herself in a submissive role, more or less as part of her heritage.

"Italian men like to dominate," she said. "It's something that I have felt at times in my life."

10

THE WANNABEES

As is frequently the case with celebrities who make it suddenly, a number of important changes occur almost simultaneously, confusing the actual sequence of events and causing trivialities to overshadow consequentialities and inconsequentialities to diminish important events.

ITEM: *Madonna* album debuts in 1982, begins to catch on in late 1984, and hits 2.8 million in 1985.

ITEM: *Like a Virgin* album sells over 2 million copies in the United States in December 1984 alone.

ITEM: *Vision Quest*, with Madonna's cameo appearance as singer, opens in early 1985, featuring two of Madonna's songs, including "Crazy for You." Retitled *Crazy for You!* the picture is rereleased in Britain on the strength of Madonna's appearance.

ITEM: *Desperately Seeking Susan* opens in March 1985 to great reviews and critical acclaim for its two stars.

ITEM: The "Madonna image" becomes a viable commodity, establishing her as a true "celebrity personality," with accessories selling everywhere and establishing a cult of "wannabees"—as in "I wannabee Madonna, too!"

When her second album was released, Madonna had quite intelligently refurbished her image of tackiness and eclectic mix of funk into a more sophisticated and trendy look. Instead of parodying several types of wear, she concentrated on a focus of "materiality."

The 1983 Madonna was instantly noticeable. The costume she wore on the album cover showed her in a silk wedding dress, with strings of beads hanging from her neck and wrists, with a crucifix dangling just over her waist, and with an enormous belt buckle decorated in capital letters spelling out BOY TOY.

But the "wedding dress" was a spoof. In actuality it was a stylishly designed piece of underwear worn as a piece of outerwear. Madonna had effectively turned herself inside out to point up the "materiality"—read, "sexuality"—of the "spiritual" marriage concept.

In this year of sudden and spectacular visibility Madonna had reinvented herself in the public eye, a task she would willingly pursue in the years immediately following. Madonna would never be a frozen prototype; she would always change with the times.

The exponentially expanding number of "Madonna Wannabees" throughout the land was no accidental phenomenon; it was a very real thing. Anyone who took a careful look around could see its strange advent in a new kind of costume female teenagers were suddenly wearing.

Nubile teeners all seemed to be running around wearing T-shirts labeled VIRGIN—advertising the Madonna album *Like a Virgin* unashamedly. Teens by the hundreds were to be seen prowling through the stores looking for cross-shaped earrings and fluorescent rubber bracelets like those Madonna wore. They would look for white lace tights that they could cut off at the ankles, along with black tube skirts that they could roll down several turns at the waist to expose their belly buttons and the waistbands of their panty hose.

They could be found looking through thrift shops, scouting for bullet-proof black lace bras and corsets, which they would wear under a gauzy shirt or frowzy jacket. They found big floppy colored rags with which they could tie up their hair. As for the hair, they frazzled that and took pains to dye it so that the roots showed dark at the scalp. Just like Madonna's.

If there was any motif to the Madonna Wannabee look, it might have been this: What was inside and hidden was now to be visible and seen. What was engineered to be seen and envied was now covered up or ripped apart and patched together again. There was to be no such thing as tradition or habit; each day was a new day full of new twists and turns— a celebration of Madonna's instinct to continue to reinvent herself from day to day.

All this activity among the country's female teenagers was not lost on the community at large. Something was happening, and the arbiters of social mores wanted to know what it was. Even the prestigious and stately *New York Times* took note of the new kid on the block with a fairly extensive story about Madonna and her best-selling album, plus facets of her past and her background. The fact that she was now a million-airess had a great deal to do with media interest of course—if not *everything* to do with it.

As early as January 6, 1985, Stephen Holden wrote a piece in the Sunday *New York Times*, not only detailing the items in her *Like a Virgin* album but even analyzing her entertainment talents. Or lack of them.

"Madonna is the brassiest star to emerge so far among the new breed of singing starlets that have been spawned by music video. Wrinkling her pretty doll face into a provocative pout and exposing her bare midriff," he wrote, Madonna frequently reminded one of a 1990s version of some of the blond bombshells of the past—women like Marilyn Monroe, Jayne Mansfield, or perhaps even Jean Harlow.

He pointed out that her song "Material Girl" contained a significant statement to the effect that the man with money is always the "right man" for any woman. This idea, he said, was a close parody of the lyrics of "Diamonds Are a Girl's Best Friend," from Jule Styne's Broadway hit *Gentlemen Prefer Blondes*, originally starring Carol Channing on Broadway in 1949, but popularized on the big screen later by Marilyn Monroe.

He went on to examine Madonna's music, noting that like a great deal of what he called "new wave and disco," it too broke away from middle-class pop music of the past and indulged in the basics of rock and roll, becoming a kind of musical cartoon of self-gratification.

"Like most of today's mainstream pop idols, the world outside [Madonna's] own juvenile dreams barely exists," he wrote. "When it does come into view, it's not a place to be understood, but a jungle to be navigated."

The story pointed out that Madonna, unlike many rock stars, had rarely performed in live concert. To Holden, this demonstrated that a telegenic image was more important for a pop artist's success than a "strong live act."

The *Times* was a little late with the news, but Madonna had already planned a long, grueling, seven-week tour of the United States. It was her first of course—and it turned out to be a stunningly successful money-maker.

Reviewers otherwise occupied in Madonna's earlier years now suddenly sat up and took notice of her. They even began to analyze her work in a serious manner, point by point, detail by detail, just like *The New York Times*. And they analyzed her image, too, not once but again and again.

Time magazine took exception to the BOY TOY belt buckle she wore, pointing out that it offended almost everyone except the full-fledged Madonna Wannabees.

"Some feminists clearly feel that Madonna's self-parody as an eye-batting gold digger, notably in her song 'Material Girl,' is a joke too damaging to laugh at," the periodical pontificated. "Somebody has said that her high, thin voice, which is merely adequate for her energetic but not very demanding dance-pop songs, sounds like 'Minnie Mouse on helium.' Other detractors suggest that she is almost entirely helium, a gas-filled, lighter-than-air creation of MTV and other sinister media packagers."

After describing the tour show as being made up of the best of her singles from her first two albums, *Time* took off the gloves and waded right in:

"This is no girl group," the write-up said. "Madonna's

two backup dancers are male and masculine. But they are small and unmenacing, dressed cheerfully in hand-painted jeans and jackets, and when they frisk about the stage with Madonna, the mood is light and childish."

It described her costume of spiked boots, black fishnet tights, and miniskirt slung at hip height to reveal her trademark belly button. She wore a loose-fitting, hand-painted jacket that swung away now and then to show a lacy purple shirt and the famous black bra. It described the floppy purple rag tied around her hair.

"The costume is sexy," the review went on, "and light as she is, at five feet four and a half inches and 118 pounds, her body is lush. But her movements . . . are skipping and prancing steps, mischievous kid stuff."

The New York Times reviewed Madonna's "undulating midriff," pointing out that it had made Madonna "this year's" most talked-about new star. The numbers in the show presented Madonna, Robert Palmer wrote, as a contemporary golddigger on the disco scene—a woman who could get any man she wanted, especially a rich, fast-track high-roller.

She was proving to be more a vamp in her videos and in her concert performances, showing off new and revealing outfits and miming that sultry, come-on look she favored.

No matter how good the somewhat mundane backup band was, Madonna simply could not sing very well. Her intonation was "atrocious." Her ear was not accurate—sometimes she sang sharp, sometimes flat. Because of her rather tentative pitch and weak vocal timber, the notes she held at the ends of her phrases sounded "like they were crawling off somewhere to die." Her higher notes achieved a more attractive sound, Palmer admitted, with just a husky bit of "street-corner edginess" in evidence.

What she needed, he felt, was a visit to a good vocal coach before staging another tour. "One hopes," he concluded, "that next time she performs here, she will have learned not to toss tambourines into the air unless she's going to be able to catch them."

But the reviews were not all raps. *The Washington Post* was impressed by Madonna's dancing.

"As a dancer," Richard Harrington wrote, "Madonna

suggested a confluence of old-fashioned *Shindig*-style dancing and contemporary video choreography, with an extra dose of belly-thrusting to reflect her championing of the midriff." She was accompanied by two male dancers who also sang vocals to back up her muscular choreography.

Harrington pointed out that each song was a production number in itself, fashioned to emulate the famous Motown sound of the sixties. The concert was "a warming, aggressive extension of the static video imagery that helped make Madonna a star in the first place."

Her own image was provocative—celebrating, as she always did onstage, her own sensuousness. Vampy, flirty, but always in control, she played her role to the hilt. On "Like a Virgin," Harrington wrote, "she prowled the stage like a lioness, and several times the whirling dervish abandon of her dance seemed genuine rather than staged."

And she was always poking fun at herself as well as at the world. This was true of both "Virgin" and "Material Girl" routines. On the latter, "Madonna assumed her helium voice and camped things up delightfully, as if the best laugh is the one you can have on yourself."

It was Madonna, Harrington pointed out, "who met the challenge of her hype head-on" and succeeded as a totally professional dancer-singer in turning her massive self-confidence into "an hour's worth of pop exaltation."

The show featured a bit of dialogue, too—at least it was dialogue of a sort. One reviewer picked up a typical speech from Madonna as she wandered out into the stage carrying a huge boombox:

"Every lady has a box. My box is special. Because it makes music. But it has to be turned on."

Sometimes the lyrics explained the dance movements. For example, in doing the "Like a Virgin" number Madonna would sashay about the stage and sing "You make me feel"—hip thrust—"like a virgin"—belly roll—"touched for the very first time."

Time: "Mocking virginity, mocking sex, mocking, some might say, the solemn temple of rock 'n' roll itself."

But she topped all her numbers with "Material Girl." Carried onto the stage in a reclining position by her backup dancers, Madonna would be twirling a long rope of pearls and kidding the whole entertainment racket for what it was as she did so.

"This is," she would sing to a pop-reggae beat, "a material world. And I am"—pause—"a material girl."

Then she would sing about being available to the highest bidder, then immediately deny it outright. At the end of the number she would always pull a wad of fake banknotes out of the top of her dress and fling it out into the audience in a kind of spirited commentary on modern America.

The tour flushed out Madonna Wannabees from half the homes of America. "One Madonna after another," the *Washington Post* said about the fans of the tour at a sold-out concert at Merriweather Post Pavilion.

"Maybe the hair beneath the bow looked a bit cleaner than hers. Maybe there was less to reveal under their mesh shirts than under hers. Maybe they were indistinguishable from the 537 other girls wearing the same crucifix earrings, lace stockings, etc. Maybe their mothers were with them. None of that mattered to the Madonna faithful."

Listen to what her fans were saying as they swarmed around the theaters all across America where her show was playing. Many of them were dressed in a kind of Basic Madonna: three pairs of earrings, a green or orange bra, with straps showing, a pair of see-through lace T-shirts, eyebrow-pencil beauty marks, strand after strand of rhinestones and pearls, and layered knit skirts that fit like Saran Wrap.

"She gives us ideas," one teenager said. "It's really women's lib, not being afraid of what guys think."

"I had to tease my hair, and my mom made some of my clothes. But it's worth it. She's such a good singer."

"Yeah. She expresses herself really well."

"Our parents don't like us acting like her. But—"

"—she gets all the guys!"

"I love her. Madonna, she's so cool. She's like a great, gifted personality. She's not just sexy. She's a personality. She's what she wants to be. I mean, she affects everybody. Look, everybody wears a lot of bracelets now."

"We don't understand why all these people are trying to look like her!"

"We think it's bad for all these little kids to admire her. Did you see her movie? She was a *slut*, she *smoked*."

"We like her music—it's fantastic. She's got a great voice."

"But her life-style, as far as she portrayed it, we don't think it's good for little kids."

"We saw a girl, she must have been *seven*, in lipstick, high heels!"

"An earring bigger than I would wear. You look at them and wonder why they want to be someone else."

Yes. The phenomenon of Madonna had swept the nation—the world in fact—and it was Madonna herself who was not quite sure what to do about it. With everyone wanting to be just like her, to dress like her, to act like her, to *be* her, she was unprepared for the total adulation afforded her. And she tried to reason out in her own way why she presented this particular image to the world. As she told Denise Worrell of *Time* magazine:

> *My image to people, I think, is that I'm this brazen, aggressive young woman who has an okay voice with some pretty exciting songs, who wears what she wants to wear and says what she wants to say and who has potential as an actress.*
>
> *Sex symbol? That is such a weird question. I guess I would be perceived as that because I have a typically voluptuous body and because the way I dress accents my femininity, and because a lot of what I am about is just expressing sexual desire and not really caring what people think about it. Maybe that would make you a sex symbol, I don't know. There is a very modest side to me, too. How far away is the image from me? It's about twenty steps away.*

As for accusations of anticlerical bias because of the crucifixes and rosaries she sported in her dress, Madonna remarked:

> *I think I have always carried around a few rosaries with me. There was the turquoise-colored one that my grandmother*

had given to me a long time ago. One day I decided to wear it as a necklace. I thought, "This is kind of offbeat and interesting."

I mean, everything I do is sort of tongue-in-cheek. It's a strange blend—a beautiful sort of symbol, the idea of someone suffering, which is what Jesus Christ on a crucifix stands for, and then not taking it seriously at all. Seeing it as an icon with no religiousness attached to it. It isn't a sacrilegious thing for me. I'm not saying, "This is Jesus Christ," and I'm laughing.

I went to Catholic schools. I thought the huge crucifixes nuns wore around their necks with their habits were really beautiful. I have one like that now. I wear it sometimes, but not onstage. It's too big. It might fly up in the air and hit me in the face.

Madonna had an interesting comment to make about the BOY TOY belt buckle she wore on her album cover:

About four years ago I used to live in the East Village. I used to love hanging out at the Roxy with all the break dancers and graffiti artists and the deejays. Everybody had a tag name they would write on the wall like "Whiz Kid" or "Hi-Fi." The thing was to see how much you could "throw up" [get your name up] everywhere. It was a very territorial thing.

One day I just thought of BOY TOY, and when I threw it up on a wall, everybody said they thought it was funny too. They understood the humor of it. I can see how the rest of the world thinks I'm saying "play with me" and "I'm available to anyone." Once again, it's a tongue-in-cheek statement, the opposite of what it says.

I had BOY TOY made into a belt buckle. Then I started doing stuff outside New York City and I kept wearing the BOY TOY belt, forgetting that no one outside of the Roxy was going to get it. I don't wear it anymore, because it's just become ridiculous. I think it's funny, but not too many other people do.

Madonna had no compunction about discussing her very visible belly button. "The picture inside the dust sleeve of my first album has me, like, in this Betty Boop pose with my belly button showing. Then, when people reviewed the album, they kept talking about my cute belly button."

I started thinking about it, and I said, "Yeah, well, I do like my belly button." I think there are other unobvious places on the body that are sexy, and the stomach is kind of innocent. I don't have a really flat stomach. I sort of have a little girl's stomach. It's round, and the skin is smooth and it's nice. I like it.

It was all coming together for Madonna. She had made it. Her life would never be the same again. In many ways that was fine with her. In one way she had lost something that she would never be able to regain.

Her independence and her freedom.

11
THE BRAT (what it)

He was cast as Jeff Spicolli in the film *Fast Times at Ridgemont High*—a character who was the archetypal spaced-out, antiheroic, eighties goofball. His real name was Sean Penn, a twenty-one-year-old actor. After making his auspicious debut in *Fast Times* in 1982, Penn suddenly found himself on call for numerous roles in varying degrees of theatrical importance.

From the beginning Penn was the prototypical 1980s actor. His birthright was impeccable. He came from a completely theatrical family: his father, Leo Penn, was a talented actor/director, working mostly in television, but occasionally on the big screen; his mother was Eileen Ryan, a former actress. Even his brother, Chris Penn, six years younger, appeared eventually in *Footloose* and *The Wild Life* soon after his brother Sean's debut.

Graduating from Santa Monica High School in 1978, Penn first studied drama with Peggy Fuery. She once said of him, "What inspired me was how concentrated Sean was." Always dedicated to Method acting—that is, in *becoming* the person he portrayed—Penn drove some directors up the wall with his antics, and inspired others to accolades.

Richard Rosenthal, who directed *Bad Boys*, Penn's second picture, said, "He's by far the most talented actor of his generation." A sweeping statement, that, and unremitting in its admiration.

Even on the set of *Fast Times*, Amy Heckerling, his director, remembered, "Sean stayed in character between takes."

Because of Penn's predilection for always being "on" and "in the role," Rosenthal found himself treading the thin line between serenity and big trouble in his dealings with his somewhat flaky actor.

During the filming of *Bad Boys*, a story of teenage delinquents in a juvenile prison, Rosenthal and the actors went out to view the Chicago police in action—they were shooting on location in the Windy City—in order to learn a little bit about the reality of police procedure to lend authenticity to their make-believe. Accompanying the police on a real hotel raid, they were standing around with a group of officers when the door opened.

Several policemen came in quickly, mistakenly identifying the film people as part of the rounded-up criminals. They told the actors to raise their hands.

"I complied," Rosenthal said, "but for Sean this was an opportunity to find out what it's like for a gang member to take on a cop."

He turned on the cop, who, as Rosenthal expressed it, "was the size of a small condo," and mouthed off at him.

"Fuck you!" was the least of Penn's comment.

"The cop picked Sean up and threw him into a wall," Rosenthal related. "[Sean's] nose was almost broken, but later he told me it was at that moment he finally made the transition to becoming the character."

A woman reporter wrote about Penn, "His is a face that a camera loves more than the naked eye. With its oddly compacted angles, small, thoughtful mouth, and quick bright eyes, it is a fascinating face, but not a conventionally handsome one. Far more valuable, for Penn's purposes, is the fact that it has a quirky masculine appeal not unlike Spencer Tracy's—a spiky toughness offset by humor and intelligence."

Amy Heckerling put it this way, "There's something very identifiable about him, and yet very serious at the same time."

Whatever was his special appeal, Penn began getting good parts. He soon appeared in *Racing with the Moon*, in which he played an attentive, clean-cut, and attractive young lover. Later on, in *The Falcon and the Snowman*, he was a dope runner and part-time traitor.

During the filming of *Racing with the Moon*, in which Penn starred with Elizabeth McGovern, he and McGovern carried on an offscreen romance in tandem with the romance in the script. The press scented sexual overtones and played it to the hilt.

McGovern recalled, "As soon as I met him, he fixed me with those piercing eyes that ripped into my heart." She went on, "I tried for it not to happen. But I just couldn't fight those blue eyes."

Even earlier, on the *Fast Times* set, Pam Springsteen, Bruce Springsteen's sister, became a media item linked with Sean Penn. He was also seen around and about with actress Susan Sarandon. In all three cases these "media" romances finally wound up in the trash can, vanishing into the limbo where such visible nonaffairs find their final resting place.

During the filming of *Racing with the Moon*, Penn's on-set image began to a sharpen up a bit. The man who had been fuzzy in detail for some time now could be seen more clearly in focus. He was slowly turning into what would later be called a crusty brat—the latter word used to group together a number of Penn's friends and fellow actors in the collective and seemingly affectionate epithet Brat Pack.

On one occasion Penn threatened a photographer, Janet Gough, who had come onto the set to promote the picture. Gough recalled, "He told me he had a water pistol and if I didn't leave, he was going into the men's room, fill the pistol with urine, and come out and squirt me."

The particular action that brought Penn's character into question was a long and ongoing quarrel with the two producers of the pictures: the formidable Sherry Lansing and Stanley Jaffe. In an interview published later on, the two producers reviled Penn for "unprofessional conduct"—a catchall term covering everything from yawning on the set to malfeasance in performance.

This "unprofessionalism" occurred not during the making of the film but afterward. The focus of their polemic seemed to be that when *People* magazine wanted to generate a revealing story of Penn's off-screen "romance" with his costar Elizabeth McGovern, Penn refused to comply. The two producers accused him in public of trying to sabotage the promotion of the film.

So the image of "brat" was superimposed over the image of zonked-out goofball. All of which annoyed Penn. He was newly into his craft and wanted reassurance from everyone that he was a serious artist. Instead of that, he was becoming known as a flake and a weirdo. *That* was just what he did *not* need.

It was certainly not surprising, then, that at about the time Madonna burst onto the entertainment scene, Sean Penn would be interested in seeing exactly what made her tick. After all, she had twisted the tiger's tail with her Catholic jibes, with her sexual innuendos, with her "boy toy" catchphrase.

During the filming of Madonna's "Material Girl" video, she was surprised to learn that there was a stranger on the set asking to see her. The stranger was the actor Sean Penn. Madonna was, of course, stunned. She knew of him; she had seen his pictures. She was enthralled to think that a *celebrity* should be interested in her.

"He was somebody whose work I'd admired, and I think he felt the same way [about my work]. I never thought in a million years I would meet him."

Yet she understood their obvious compatibility of course. "He had a rebellious bad-boy image—the same as I did, only for a girl."

But—romance? The details become distorted at this distance, but their meeting was typical of a Madonna love affair. It did not start out with bells ringing in anyone's ears. It was—

"I don't feel swept off my feet," Madonna reported. "He's wild, though. He'll probably die young. We have so much in common—we were born one day apart—and have such similar temperaments. I feel like he is my brother or something. In fact, when I squint my eyes, he almost looks like my father when he was younger."

Penn later confessed, "I just remember her saying, 'Get out! Get out! Get out!'"

Madonna did not even remember that.

To follow Penn's recollections for a moment, he remembered what happened *after* he had met her. "I was over at a friend's house, and he had a book of quotations. He picked it up and turned to a random page and read as follows: 'She had the innocence of a child and the wit of a man.' I looked at my friend, and he just said, 'Go get her.'"

The romance between them—for such it was to be, complete with happy ending and unhappy sequel—began slowly. They did not date exclusively for several months, and yet they spent a great deal of their spare time together.

Although Madonna was taken with Penn's smoldering and antipathetic charm, she held back just a bit. Yes, she had always liked dark, brooding men with hot tempers. Yes, she had always liked the darker side of life.

But she joked about Penn's attractions by saying that she had always been interested in "small furry animals with big eyes that stay up at night and hang off the trees by their tails. Maybe that's what attracted me to Sean!"

Nevertheless, joke or no joke, the affair burgeoned. The wooing of Madonna by Penn, oddly enough, took on the typical structure of the wooing of any Jill by any Jack.

ITEM: Penn knew how infatuated Madonna was with her resemblance to Marilyn Monroe. When she visited the West Coast, Penn took her to see the actress's grave. "Joe DiMaggio's rose was there," Madonna recalled breathlessly. "He really loved her."

ITEM: They made a lot out of the fact that their birthdays were only one day apart. It was, they thought, a sure sign of a good-luck linkage between the two of them.

ITEM: On Madonna's upcoming "Virgin" tour Penn visited her in Miami, in Santa Barbara, and in Detroit.

ITEM: Both Madonna's and Penn's fortunes seemed to be on the rise simultaneously. And that meant that they were obviously meant for one another.

Some friends and acquaintances were just a little surprised that these two should fancy each other. Susan Seidelman, who had inadvertently propelled Madonna to fame by casting her in *Desperately Seeking Susan,* mused, "I don't think she needed Sean in opportunistic ways. Movie people are always beating her down." Besides, Seidelman decided, "She could have anyone she wants. If it was just for the sake of getting married, she could marry somebody richer, better looking, and more politically connected than Sean." And so, Seidelman reasoned perversely, "It's got to be love."

As for Madonna, she put it this way: "We have so much in common, [Sean] is almost like my brother. He's really smart and he knows a lot. He's also willing to play the outsider or nerd rather than the hero that everybody likes."

Besides, "his temperament is also similar to mine." But, mainly, Madonna admitted, "I am attracted to ambitious people, so you've got to take what comes with that."

Because they were both in the business of entertainment, and to be an entertainer meant one must spend much of one's time marketing oneself, exigencies occurred that split them apart rather than welded them together.

Penn had just signed on to make a new film, *At Close Range.* And Madonna had just signed on for a gigantic tour of the United States—twenty-eight cities to play to three hundred thousand fans—to flog her *Like a Virgin* album.

And so in April 1985 the separation came that would keep them physically apart for something like three months. Madonna's "Virgin" tour opened in Seattle, Washington, and Penn started to work on his new film in Atlanta, Georgia.

The media began fine-tuning "affairs" for Madonna once again. She was connected with a long string of men, both in the entertainment business and out of it. Prince. Billy Idol. Don Johnson. David Lee Roth. John F. Kennedy, Jr. Huh? Right! John F. Kennedy, Jr.

Prince? Sure. She had met him on tour in San Francisco. Billy Idol? Sure, she had once considered writing a song with him because he and she were both "white and plastic and blond." Don Johnson? Sure. He wanted to make a record with her. David Lee Roth? Yeah. She had once invited him to a party. John F. Kennedy, Jr.? Why not? Boy George had introduced Madonna to John-John when they both attended his New York birthday party. The media added the ghost of JFK to the ghost of Monroe/Madonna and saw in their crystal balls a very good thing indeed!

Came to nothing.

The geographical gap between Madonna and Sean Penn during their summer apart was quite easily bridged by the judicious use of the air-transportation industry. In fact Madonna was able to fly down to visit Penn in the South several times during the height of her tour.

It was apparently during one of their get-togethers that summer that Sean Penn got the great idea: Let's get married.

"I was jumping up and down on the bed, performing one of my morning rituals, and all of a sudden Sean got this look in his eye. I felt like I knew what he was thinking."

Madonna told him, "Whatever you're thinking, I'll say yes to."

And that was Penn's chance. "He proposed," Madonna said.

It didn't take long for the famous *m* word to get out: "marriage!" *That* story surfaced in the primary gossip source of the country—the New York *Daily News*. It was a break published first by columnist "Suzy" on June 24, and it grew to gigantic proportions. Even the date of the supposed nuptials became common knowledge: sometime in August after Penn finished shooting *At Close Range*. Some wise journalist consulted the stars and decided it was going to be on Madonna's birthday—and that was accurate to a decimal point.

With the focus on Sean Penn and the press, the rest of the media woke up, and soon the area around the location shoot was swarming with news hawks.

On June 30 somebody discovered that the two celebs were together in a Nashville, Tennessee, hotel. It was not long before a pair of free-lance British journalists—Laurence Cottrell and Ian Markham-Smith by name—began to tail the two of them. Penn immediately spotted them and began to sound off.

Words did not deter the British reporters. They were far more determined and far more spirited than their American counterparts. They continued their grim pursuit of the pair, to the growing rage of Sean Penn.

Soon Penn resorted to his usual style, allegedly throwing a rock at Cottrell. He then—again allegedly—wrenched Cottrell's camera away from him and flailed the journalist with it, on his arms, upper body, and back. The details are obfuscated now, but apparently no one was seriously hurt. However, the journalists called in the law, and Penn was arrested.

Eventually he was released on a five-hundred-dollar bond. He wound up leaving Tennessee with a suspended sentence hanging over his head.

Suddenly everyone was reading about Madonna and Sean Penn.

Even publishers.

Even photography agencies.

What has been called the Battle of the Soft Porn began in reality with Bob Guccione, the publisher of *Penthouse*. Suddenly he had on his desk piles of photographs of Madonna in the nude—pictures that she had posed for during her largely starvation days in the East Village when she had stripped down not only for life classes in drawing but also for photographers as well.

"A great number of Madonna nudes had surfaced all at once, and we had first choice," Guccione bragged. "They came from many different sources—photography teachers and their students, amateurs, and professionals."

In the Chicago offices of *Playboy*, Hugh Hefner was also looking at piles of pictures of Madonna in the buff. With the photos surfacing at the same time that the announcement of the impending wedding was making all the columns, it became a race between *Playboy* and *Penthouse* to show Madonna in the nude *first*.

Guccione wired Madonna, offering her a million dollars to pose for a new exclusive *Penthouse* session. Madonna turned her back on the whole thing and left the details to a publicity agent.

Who said, spiritedly, "Madonna has absolutely nothing to say."

Thinking he might get some reaction out of Sean Penn, Guccione sent advances of the issue to the actor.

Madonna privately seethed at that move. She considered

it a blow below the belt. And she was streetwise enough to be able to distinguish between ordinary professional competition and downright gratuitous nastiness.

In the Race of the Soft Porn Biggies, Hefner won—and on July 10, 1985, the whole world finally saw what Madonna looked like—all over.

Actually the pictures were pretty tame.

"When people saw them, they thought, 'What's the big deal here?' " Madonna reported, quite accurately. "But I can't say I wasn't devastated by the experience."

Nevertheless Sean Penn showed strength of character in the incident. "Look," he told Madonna, "this is all going to blow over."

It still hurt. Bad. "Nobody wants their skeletons to come out of the closet," Madonna said. "No matter how successful you want to be, you can never, ever anticipate that kind of attention—the grand scale of it all.

"The thing that annoyed me the most was the fact that, for the first time in several years of careful planning and knowing what was going to happen, I felt really out of control. It took me by surprise. I reminded me of the time when I was a little girl at school and the nuns used to come along and lift your dress up in front of everybody to check what color panties you were wearing. It's embarrassing because you're just not ready for it and you feel so exposed.

"Now I look back and I feel silly that I ever got so upset, but I remember feeling that same, end-of-the-world feeling the day my stepmother told me I couldn't wear stockings to school. I cried for hours and thought I wouldn't live through the next day. You think it's the end of the world, and then one day it's not."

Her first public appearance after the nudie fiasco found Madonna performing before ninety thousand people in Philadelphia's JFK Stadium to raise money for Live Aid.

Bette Midler introduced Madonna to the crowd, categorizing her snippishly as "a woman who pulled herself up by her bra straps and has been known to let them down occasionally."

Madonna wasn't going to let that remark go unanswered.

She came right back in her sarcastic fashion. "I ain't taking *shit* off today!" she told the audience with a toss of the head.

Penn was with Madonna, holding her hand backstage. It took guts for her to show up at a live performance with so much of the public suddenly hostile to her. The fact that she appeared without any pretense made her even more popular with her true fans. In fact the appearance definitely bolstered her name and image among both friends and foes.

But many were hostile who had once been friendly. The mayor of her hometown—Bay City in Michigan—went back on his decision to honor Madonna with the Key to the City. "It would not be in good taste to give it to her now," he told the press primly.

Much of the negativism came from the feminists. They were in full cry now, reminding their followers that the only way to compete in a so-called man's world was to try to act like a man, even dress like one. Madonna had, of course, demonstrated that there was no point in denying your own true nature when you could be smart and feminine at the same time. And sexy too. Was sex a crime?

"They said that I'd set women back thirty years. Well, in the fifties women weren't ashamed of their bodies. They luxuriated in their sexuality and they were very strong in their femininity. Women aren't like men. I've only recently come to understand that to some women I represent a kind of liberation for females. I give young women strength and hope. So in that respect I feel my behavior, my art, is feminist."

Right on! her fans urged. Right on!

12
Tiffany's—with a Dash of Flash

The pen-and-ink drawing showed two people who could have been anyone standing—à la Grant Wood—next to an upright lawn rake, a tiny mailbox, and a stylized Middle America cottage behind them. The man, dressed in jeans and a leather jacket, held a can of beer in his right hand; the woman wore a cut-off blouse with a bare midriff featuring her navel, below which a belt buckle spelled out the words SEAN TOY as it helped hold up her cut-off shorts.

On the other side the invitation read:

Please Come to Sean and Madonna's
Birthday Party on the Sixteenth of August
Nineteen Eighty-Five
The Celebration Will Commence at Six O'Clock P.M.
Please Be Prompt or You Will Miss Their
Wedding Ceremony
The Need for Privacy and a Desire to Keep You Hanging
Prevents the Los Angeles Location from Being Announced
Until One Day Prior*
R.S.V.P. by August 3 to:

Clyde Is Hungry Productions
6521 Leland Way   Hollywood, CA 90028
(203) 460-6208
* Please include a phone number where you can be reached.

Prior to the wedding, of course, both prospective bride and groom had been invited to prenuptial parties—the likes of which, at least in their scope, content, and commitment, are not generally enjoyed by the average person.

In July 1985 Madonna was invited to a wedding shower held in the Upper East Side Manhattan apartment of Nancy Huang, a friend of Madonna's (second album) record producer, Nile Rodgers.

Present were a dozen or so firm friends of Madonna's, including singer Alannah Currie of the Thompson Twins, and actress Mariel Hemingway. The gift boxes for Madonna contained lingerie, a quilt, a sequined push-button phone, jewelry, and other goodies.

For diversion and amusement there were a half-dozen male friends in attendance, dressed in drag especially for the occasion.

But that wasn't the only celebration. Two days before the wedding Madonna and ten friends held an old-fashioned bachelorette party at the Tropicana, a mud-wrestling club in probably the seediest and tackiest area of seedy, tacky Hollywood. In dark glasses, no makeup, and hair in a tight librarian's bun, Madonna sat and cheered two wrestlers who were making each other miserable in the slop and mud.

Just before the wedding Sean Penn had a similar, but totally unlike celebration—an old-fashioned stag party. The chief entertainer at the affair was a stripper named Kitten Natividad, whose measurements were an incredible 42-24-36. The party was held in a private room above Hollywood's Roxy nightclub.

Present were Chris Penn, actors Harry Dean Stanton, David Keith, Tom Cruise, and Robert Duvall, with Cameron Crowe, the screenwriter of *Fast Times at Ridgemont High*. They all watched in disbelief as Kitten Natividad began peeling her outer wear off to a blasting tape of "Material Girl."

When Harry Dean Stanton arrived late, Penn picked up Kitten's blouse and said to Stanton, "See what you missed?"

With that, according to Kitty's story, Penn shoved Stanton's face straight into her bust. The stripper said she did not mind one iota.

"Sometimes I do," she admitted, "but it was Sean's night, and he could have done whatever he wanted to. That was about as wild as he got."

Kitten's assessment of Sean Penn was along these lines: "He's a very nice guy. He reminds me of a little boy, like he's eight years old and he's got so many cookies he doesn't know what to do with them."

Thanks to the booze, "they were all pretty buzzed," the stripper observed. "Sean," she said, "was feeling no pain. But he didn't fall on his face or anything. When he talked, he made sense."

As for the wedding itself, the "secret location" of the nuptials of Madonna and Sean Penn was revealed the day before the affair: It was the six-and-a-half-million-dollar estate of a producer, real estate developer, and friend of the Penn family, Dan Unger. The estate was situated in Malibu, California, on a high promontory called Point Dume.

At the entrance to the estate a regiment of security guards dressed in blue blazers helped perform an identification check on all the wedding guests as they entered the sacred precincts.

And tight security it was indeed. Early that morning—at one thirty A.M.—a man dressed in camouflage uniform, blackened face à la World War II commando, was discovered hiding in the bushes somewhere on the vast estate. He turned out to be a photographer from Italy! His camera was seized, his film destroyed, and he himself was ejected summarily and no doubt told to rediscover Italy.

Above the estate a half-dozen helicopters for hire, loaded with photographers, all of whom had been excluded from invitations to the wedding itself, churned up the air and swooped up and down to view the goings-on from above. It was the nearest any of them got to the actual proceedings.

Invited to the wedding were 220 select friends, associates,

and so on—among them Madonna's seven brothers and sisters, her seventy-three-year-old grandmother, Sean Penn's family, and a group of friends.

For the bride and groom there were Rosanna Arquette, Madonna's costar in *Desperately Seeking Susan,* Christopher Walken, Carrie Fisher, Andy Warhol, Diane Keaton, Timothy Hutton, and Tom Cruise.

Cruise was a member of the Hollywood Brat Pack, a group that included Timothy Hutton, Penn's best friend, Emilio Estevez (one of Martin Sheen's acting sons).

The guest list included such luminaries as *Late Night's* David Letterman, superagent Stan Kamen, Cher, who showed up in spiky purple hair, record mogul David Geffen, and actress Carol Kane, among scores of others.

It took security more than an hour to admit the guests, who filed past the legion of reporters and photographers kept at bay outside the gates and then were paced through a complicated security labyrinth devised to keep out any prowlers and led on to a poolside setting that overlooked the Pacific Ocean, where they could relax.

Far below in the distance, as the setting sun sank lower and lower in the west, the guests could hear the Pacific surf pounding against the sheer rock bluff that plunged down from the estate.

And in the air above, stirring up the atmosphere, the six helicopters continued their restless surveillance of the ground festivities below. In plain view of the pilots and photographers zooming about was what *Time* magazine described as "an obscene greeting" that someone—guess who—had lettered out plainly in the sand at the bottom of the cliff.

Outside the Unger estate, the hundred uninvited journalists and photographers hung about expectantly, ogling and snapping shots of those celebrities lucky enough to be invited to the wedding. The big game here was to be the first to spot Madonna and Sean Penn as they arrived at the heavily guarded gate and made their way through the crowd.

Amazingly enough, the bride and groom never showed up. How they got in is their own secret. Did they time their arrival to avoid the early birds of the media gang? Did they know of an alternate route of entry? The answers to these questions are buried in entertainment history.

According to the *Los Angeles Times*, the original security plan to prevent hordes of fans from invading the Unger estate was to instruct guests to assemble at a spot at least a mile from the gates, where they would be driven by bus to the house itself. However, the real address was given out the day before, and the media found out in time to put in their appearance.

Sean Penn acted in character throughout the days preceding the celebration, playing the "reluctant" public figure. Even at his famous stag party, he had opted to pass by photographers, his face hidden by a towel or blanket.

Just prior to the wedding, the bride and groom had stayed at Madonna's two-bedroom apartment in the Hollywood Hills. As a cost-of-living footnote to history, *People* magazine noted that the rent was $1,350 a month.

The wedding ceremony itself went off without a hitch.

At six thirty the bride and groom appeared as if by magic. The groom was dressed in a double-breasted Gianni Versace suit that he had purchased off the rack a week earlier on Beverly Hills's famous Rodeo Drive.

The bride was dressed in a strapless Cinderella gown created by her tour designer and video-image maker, Marlene Stewart. Her French-twist hairdo was covered by a black bowler hat draped in cream-colored tulle, with a single long earring and an antique pearl bracelet substituting for her discarded trademark crucifixes.

Across her dress, draped like a beauty contestant's sash, was a silver-and-pink silk metallic net, dripping with encrusted jewels, pearls, and dried roses.

"We wanted a fifties feeling," Stewart said later, "something Grace Kelly might have worn."

The bride walked down the grassy aisle on the arm of her father as the music played "Moments of Love." When finally she let go of Silvio Ciccone's elbow, she said to him, " 'Bye, Dad.''

During the ceremonies the couple was flanked only by the best man, director James Foley (who made Penn's *At Close*

Range) in a dark-green linen suit, and the maid of honor, Madonna's sister Paula Ciccone. Judge John Merrick conducted a five-minute ceremony in which the couple exchanged vows.

Penn then lifted his wife's veil and, as the theme from *Chariots of Fire* echoed about on the grassy bluff overlooking the now-dark Pacific, planted a kiss on her lips, at which there was a standing ovation and a cacophony of resounding huzzahs.

At this point the area was surrounded by hurrying waiters rushing about with trays of Cristal champagne and sushi. *Madame Butterfly*, by Malcolm McLaren, sounded from the loudspeakers. The guests began milling about and drinking champagne amid an incessant rumble of chatter.

Then, magically, on a balcony high above them, the newlyweds appeared like Romeo and Juliet. Sean Penn took the opportunity to toast "the most beautiful woman in the world" and then hammed it up most Pennishly by diving under Madonna's flowing skirts and coming up like a successful pearl diver clenching her red garter between his teeth. In the end Madonna's bouquet went sailing down over the edge straight into the targeted hands of her bridesmaid sister, Paula.

And that was that.

The bride and groom danced their wedding dance to Sarah Vaughan's "I'm Crazy About the Boy," and later on Sean Penn showed off some of his rather wild *Saturday Night Fever* steps to an enthusiastic group of cheering wedding guests.

The motif of the wedding was "Like a Virgin" white— and to carry it out, a blazing white tent trimmed with white bunting covered scores of tables set about on the tennis court near the house. At the center of each table was placed a modern version of Cinderella's slipper: a gold-and-jewel-encrusted spike-heeled shoe on a brocaded cushion. There were even votive candles that shimmered in reflection off the crystal champagne flutes.

Everybody crowded into the white-carpeted open-air tent to indulge in a three-course feast prepared by Spago Restaurant, including lobster ravioli, rack of lamb, swordfish, baked potatoes stuffed with sour cream and caviar, and a five-tiered hazelnut wedding cake with sugar flowers.

In addition there were special favorites from chef Wolf-
gang Puck—dishes like curried oysters from his Chinoise
on Main Street, and Spago's signature small pizzas. One
course was even prepared from fish specially flown in from
Hawaii.

As Madonna moved over to the cake, she turned to wedding guest Cher and asked, "Hey, you've done this before.
Do you just cut one piece, or do you have to slice up the
whole thing?"

Cher's response was not recorded. It didn't matter much
anyway. Madonna paid little attention to any kind of advice—
even requested advice. She cut the first piece of cake and
handed the knife to Penn. When he cut his, they threw hand-
fuls of icing and cream into each other's faces.

Anything to make the wedding really zingy.

In another room of the house the wedding gifts had begun to accumulate. There were exceptional goodies, including
an antique jukebox with twenty-four of Madonna's favorite
oldies from Mo Ostin, chairman of—what else?—Warner Bros.
Records. There was a 1912 antique silver tea service from John
Daly, producer of Sean Penn's latest film, *The Falcon and the
Snowman*. The promised twelve-piece china setting in Madonna's registered Tiffany pattern, courtesy *Playboy*, never appeared, and it was just as well, since Madonna had threatened
to return any such peace offering "in pieces."

As the evening wore on, the guests moved onto the elaborate parquet dance floor that had been set up over the tennis
courts. It was lit with pink floodlights. There was no live band
to do the entertaining, but instead disc jockey Terence Toy
spun disco tunes, opening up with a swing-era tape, then
moved on to livelier fare—Motown's greatest dance tunes and,
in spite of being warned in advance not to play any Madonna
stuff, her own "Into the Groove," and later, "Lucky Star."
When reproved for his double lapse later, Toy snapped primly:
"I *didn't* play 'Like a Virgin'!"

Madonna was seen boogying with her usual enthusiasm,
even, as *People* magazine reported, "lifting her layered skirt
during one fast-moving number to reveal a flowered-brocade
slip underneath."

The groom was not about to be outdone by his dancing wife. He grabbed Timothy Hutton, his best pal, and began capering about with him in a mock step that featured more speed and athletic energy than terpsichorean skill.

In the end Penn jumped on to Hutton piggyback style, and Hutton circled around the dance floor among the guests until he finally collapsed into a heap with Penn as the guests cheered loudly.

When DJ Terence Toy exhausted himself, a second of three backup disc jockeys took over, keeping couples on the expansive dance floor.

Meanwhile heavy security prowled the perimeters of the estate, keeping paparazzi away from the restricted area. Apparently interlopers had given up; even the choppers had vanished when darkness settled in.

About ten o'clock the party began to dissolve. "It was all very intimate, except for those obnoxious helicopters," said Susan Seidelman.

Another guest nodded. "A very classy affair. Like Tiffany's, with just a dash of flash."

Martin Burgoyne, a longtime friend of Madonna's, was asked what he thought about the chances of the marriage between Madonna and Sean Penn.

"The other relationships," he said, "weren't right because they weren't fifty-fifty. This one is. Neither one of them is in control; she can learn from him, and he can learn from her."

Already, the press was rumoring, Madonna was getting set to sign with Disney Productions for a kidnap film and was said to be shopping around for a joint movie project to do with her new husband.

In fact Madonna had given herself, as a wedding present, a brand-new midnight-blue Mercedes to drive—at the cost of forty-four thousand dollars—and she and the groom were soon making plans to buy a spacious estate in Malibu for a secluded newlyweds' nest.

Asked facetiously whether or not he was going to put up a fence around the new place, Penn answered in character, "A fence, nothing! We're going to have *gun towers*."

Believe him.

When it was all over and done, Madonna made a comment about the whole thing: "It was almost too much. I mean, I didn't think I was going to be getting married with thirteen helicopters flying over my head. It turned into a circus. In the end I was laughing. You couldn't have written it in a movie. No one would have believed it. It was like a Busby Berkeley musical."

The theatrical aspect of the wedding did not abate even at midnight. By that time Madonna had not only celebrated her wedding, but her twenty-seventh birthday as well. The bride and groom were then escorted to a chauffeured limousine and driven several miles away to the Penn household, where they spent their wedding night.

And, at midnight, the *second* day of festivities technically began. *Now* it was time to celebrate Sean Penn's twenty-fifth birthday!

13

THE SHANGHAI GESTURE

When the Beatles broke up in the seventies, the four men all went their separate ways. George Harrison eventually found himself back in the film business as a producer. In the late seventies he teamed up with Denis O'Brien, an American banker, to form a production company called HandMade Films.

The initial reason for the creation of HandMade was to help bail out the Monty Python group, who had put everything they had into a film called *The Life of Brian*. Because it was an irreverent spoof on religion—worse, on Christianity!—HandMade almost immediately lost all its original backers, who, it appeared, did not relish taking on the entire Western Hemisphere in a religious bout.

With HandMade behind *Brian*, the film was finished and released. By 1979 it was deemed a proven hit, and HandMade was a going concern. Soon it was seeking other properties to make. By the middle eighties the firm had released eleven films, including *Time Bandits*, *The Missionary*, *Privates on Parade*, and *A Private Function*.

Harrison more or less remained a partner, but definitely a silent partner as opposed to a vocal one. It was O'Brien who did most of the front work and carried on the promotion and marketing.

In 1986 HandMade found a promotable property in a scenario based on a novel by Tony Kendrick, an English author. The novel was titled *Faraday's Flowers,* which was certainly not the most brilliant title in the world for a story about a female missionary in China during the Depression years.

The story itself was a quasi-adventure/romance involving the woman missionary and an English expatriate—somewhat bent, to put it kindly, a sort of Oriental Rhett Butler. Somehow the gung-ho missionary and the reluctant hero manage to find adventure and love in China.

Martin Sheen, the actor, a good friend of the Penn family, was the person who first advised Madonna and Sean Penn about the existence of the script. He had an idea the newlyweds might be trying to locate a film they could do together. Sheen had worked with a television director named Jim Goddard on an American miniseries about the life of President John F. Kennedy. Goddard had other excellent television credits: He had made the acclaimed television adaptation of the stage production of Charles Dickens's *Nicholas Nickleby.* He had the script in hand.

Sheen recommended Madonna to Goddard, and Goddard to Madonna, as it were. Goddard had discussed the casting with the author of the original novel, and Kendrick had thought the use of Madonna might be the making of the film.

"It's a brilliant piece of casting," he said. "On the surface Madonna's character is a shy, uptight missionary, but it turns out she's not as straightlaced as all that."

Of course the Penn family hovered over the script, too, and it was Sean Penn who read it with something else in mind.

"He really liked the male role," Madonna said, "so we looked at each other and thought, 'Maybe this would be a good one to do together.' "

Talking it over, Madonna and Penn found similarities between the script—the film would be titled *Shanghai Surprise,* and not *Faraday's Flowers*—and the script of *The African Queen,* in which Humphrey Bogart and Katharine Hepburn combined action-adventure with sophisticated romance to create an acclaimed film classic.

"We were both setting ourselves up for a challenge," Madonna admitted, "the challenge of being married and working together. A lot of people said it was a sure way to end a relationship and that we'd be getting divorced afterward."

Nevertheless, in spite of the warnings, the two decided to make the film together. In fact, to fit into the role of the girl missionary—named Gloria—Madonna turned in her image of the wild street girl and wore her hair long and wavy and blond, almost in reminiscence of the prototypical Golden Age movie queen.

So, in January 1986, Madonna and Sean Penn flew to China to film the picture about Shanghai in the 1930s. It was impossible now to work in China, and the film company settled on shooting the location stuff in Hong Kong and Macao. However, the Penns were permitted to visit Shanghai as tourists, and did so to get the flavor of China before going before the cameras.

"We arrived [in Shanghai] in the middle of the night," Madonna recalled, "but we couldn't sleep, so we ended up walking around the streets on this cold morning. It was still dark, and the streets were filled with people doing their traditional, slow-motion t'ai-chi exercises. It was so dreamlike."

Incredibly enough, none of the people knew who Madonna or Sean Penn was. "I loved that," Madonna said, "and because I had blond hair, they thought I was a Martian from outer space."

Hong Kong was the next stop—where the work would begin. By the time the Penns and their entourage stepped off the ferry, a huge mass of international journalists had assembled to interview the two celebrities. However, Madonna and her husband clammed up and refused to speak a word.

Instead Jim Goddard, the director, was forced to tell the throng of writers that the film would be an "action-packed love and adventure story." Not much to give writers hungry for a story of two newlywed celebrities. Nor was it the greatest way for a pair of such celebrities to treat the assembled media of the English-speaking world in China.

Shooting began the next day. To quote Madonna about

the making of the picture, "It was downhill from the second day." It became immediately evident to the two Penns that Jim Goddard was out of his depth.

"We wanted it to be a period film," Madonna said. "Goddard wanted to shoot it fast without any production values. It was like a bad music video."

Goddard had had sufficient television experience, but apparently it wasn't really enough to allow him to make the transition to the big screen.

More was worrying Madonna than Goddard's so-called inability to make a creditable film.

"The truth is," she admitted, "Sean wasn't supposed to do the film. He didn't want to do [it]. But he also didn't want to spend four months away from me." In a way her admission contradicted her earlier statement about the project, but so what?

There was more. Madonna was having king-sized collywobbles about her own theatrical talents.

"I had all these feelings of insecurity," she recalled. "I kept thinking, 'I'll be a terrible actress and [Sean] won't love me anymore.'"

She need not have worried.

"But Sean is a very giving actor. He never makes you feel like you're not adding up a scene. That's his main thing when he's making a movie. He makes it work for whoever's in the scene with him. Strangely enough, we never got along better."

But there was still a great deal of coping to do. It was Hong Kong itself that had become the antagonist, the challenge that had to be met and bested.

"We were in a very foreign country working with a Chinese crew, and there were communication problems. I had to keep walking around in thin cotton blouses in very cold weather. There were big black rats underneath our trailers, and people were always coming down with food poisoning. I kept saying, 'I can't wait till I can look back on all this.' It was a survival test—all the odds were against us."

Since Hong Kong did not look like Shanghai in the thirties, the film crew had to select the sleaziest and most despicable slums in the area for atmosphere. And there they found themselves at the mercy of the Chinese gangsters who ruled the slums. The mob's muscle knew exactly what to do to hold up shooting and to squeeze every last dollar from the "white faces" invading their turf.

"We were at this one location for eighteen hours because they'd blocked the only exit," Madonna recalled, "and this guy wanted fifty thousand dollars to move. That went on every day, and nobody would help us."

In spite of the Chinese gangs the slum scenes were finally finished, and the film crew moved over to Macao to finish up the location shooting. Macao was a port city surrounded by a billion Chinese neighbors. The city had been founded by Portuguese traders in 1557.

It was in Macao that the real action began—action that was not really in the script of *Shanghai Surprise* at all, but that sprang instead from the hearts and souls of the Penns. In fact, from the moment they hit Macao, they were the center of controversy. Macao was jumping. Madonna found the lobby of the elegant Oriental Hotel bursting with hordes of Oriental wannabees, all leaping up and down for a look at their Western idols.

A journalist named Leonel Borralho, a reporter for the "with-it" *Hong Kong Standard* across the bay, decided he would make his fortune by photographing the couple and peddling the pictures to publications all over the world at maximum rates.

He stashed himself on the eighteenth floor of the Oriental Hotel, where the Penns were registered, and waited for them. One afternoon as Madonna and her husband got off the elevator, accompanied by their entourage of hired muscle, Borralho stepped out of a service closet and began snapping pictures of them.

One of Penn's rent-a-muscle bodyguards grabbed Borralho and dragged him over to confront Penn.

"What are you doing here?" bellowed Penn, his face flaming with rage. "Who let you in?"

Madonna was as white as a sheet. As an example, Penn turned to her, gesturing angrily. "Can't you see my wife is trembling?"

His anger took over and he made a move toward Borralho. A second muscle, seeing only trouble in the offing, pulled

Penn back. Penn turned on him in a rage. Meanwhile a third muscle yanked at Borralho's camera, trying to rip it off his neck. The strap held.

With Penn finally restrained, and Madonna subdued and pale, the hired muscle began bargaining with Borralho. If he surrendered the film he had shot, Borralho could have an exclusive interview with the couple.

That was the muscle's idea, *not* Penn's. Nor Madonna's.

When the journalist returned the next day and found that he had been conned out of his film and that there would be no photographic opportunity at all, Borralho threatened to sue the two celebrities for a million dollars. Later in the day he did indeed file suit, exactly as he had promised.

And of course the word got out. Editorials labeled Penn the Ugly American.

Work on the picture was proceeding apace, and in the same somewhat ragtag condition as the newlyweds' life in the Oriental Hotel.

"Sean and I took turns being strong and not letting things affect us too much," Madonna said. "There was a time when I was so overtaken by it, and I was crying, and he said, 'Don't worry, baby. We'll make it work.' Then in two weeks he'd be miserable and I'd be holding him up saying, 'We'll get through this.' "

The newspapers now had their targets thoroughly inked in. They were described as the Poison Penns, in typical British wordplay. The photographers continued pressuring the newlyweds for pictures, and finally the film's publicist, Chris Nixon, suggested to Penn that he and Madonna pose briefly for the paparazzi as a sort of truce—a "photo opportunity" to end all opportunities. The session might even net good results for the film itself, Nixon pointed out.

Penn almost went berserk. "Your job is not to cater to the photographers but to the film, and to me!" he yelled at the Britisher.

Nixon had his own ideas about publicity. "My job is to promote the film, and right now it *needs* the publicity!"

That hit too close to the heart of the matter not to hurt.

Penn pulled strings—ropes, more than likely—and had Nixon fired.

This was a low blow to the film crew. Liked by everyone he worked with, Nixon was a seasoned publicist and, as such, deserving they felt of better treatment than he had received from the Penns. Nevertheless he was gone now. Only the memory lingered; and a very bad one it was indeed.

Things were coming to a head. Word was deliberately leaked to George Harrison. He flew in from London to try to straighten the mess out. He visited the set one morning and delivered a rather pungent message to his celebrity stars.

After that things calmed down a bit. Madonna was asked once if she was enjoying herself in the Orient, and she shook her head.

"What? Being harassed? No. We didn't think we'd have any problem here." She pointed out that the charges against Penn were exaggerated. "That guy [Borralho] acted like a real jerk."

In addition to that, Madonna said, "I never read anything [truthful] about myself. It's always lies." She categorized her fans as "poor souls" who probably "lead such boring lives. Then they read in the paper reports detailing the lives of celebrities—their every move. They admire them and end up fantasizing about them."

When the shooting was finally over, the entire crew flew back to England with the film in the can to wrap up the shooting and edit the picture. The group arrived in London, with journalists out in full force to greet the celebs in their own inimitable fashion.

The Mercedes in which Madonna was riding became inadvertently involved in an altercation with a photographer—and of course the photographer lost in the melee. What happened was that the journalist, trying to get a picture of her and Penn, fell onto the hood of the limo, but then slid off and injured his foot when he landed on the pavement.

The headlines were predictable. "Maimed by Madonna," read the caption over a photo of the journalist. War was declared. Almost every morning the London newspapers reported nasty events surrounding the *Shanghai Surprise* stars. Some journalists complained that they had been roughed up or hosed down by muscle hired to harass them.

Then one morning, on the set, Polaroid photos of Madonna and Penn that were intended for the director's use vanished. Disappeared totally! Gone! The "Poison Penns" refused to work until the culprit who had taken them was identified. He never was. Finally Denis O'Brien, the money man, cajoled the two stars into going back to work—after five hours of filming time had been lost.

Then a female radio reporter hid in the ladies' room of the Park Lane Hotel, armed with a tape recorder, waiting to get an exclusive from Madonna. She was discovered huddled in a stall and hauled away. Another enterprising journalist even disguised herself as a Madonna look-alike to get past the guards to interview the real Madonna!

George Harrison knew he had to do something. He decided to create a meeting between the Penns and the press to iron out their differences. Someone close to Harrison put it this way: "George was trying to get Sean and Madonna to treat the press with a sense of humor."

The idea was excellent.

Its execution was the pits.

A posh press conference was held in the chic Roof Gardens, with seventy-five of London's pushiest Fleet Streeters waiting for the word from on high.

Trouble was, only Madonna showed up. Where was Sean Penn? the media types asked.

"He's busy. Working." Harrison dismissed the question as irrelevant.

The questions persisted. "Do you fight with Sean?" someone asked Madonna.

Harrison cut in. "Do you row with your wife?"

Madonna decided to come clean about George Harrison. "He's a great boss," she told the assembled journalists, "very understanding and very sympathetic. He's given me more advice on how to deal with the press than how to make movies."

Harrison grinned at the press. "You're all so busy creating a fuss, then writing about it, as if we've created it for the publicity."

"Come on, George!" someone countered. "What were you expecting?"

"We expect nonanimals," Harrison answered.

"Speaking of animals," a reporter said, "is it true that Sean was giving orders to everybody on the set?"

And so on and so forth.

"In the sixties," Harrison said, "all people could do was knock the Beatles, so I've been through it all myself." He predicted confidently that "This film [Shanghai Surprise] is going to be a box-office smash."

It would be some months before the film opened and Harrison's prediction could be proved right or wrong. Meanwhile the Penns flew home to their Malibu hideaway to continue their interrupted honeymoon. Getting home, however, did not really mellow Sean Penn out any. Soon he was up to his old tricks.

In a Los Angeles nightclub one evening in April 1986, Madonna saw her old friend David Wolinski, a songwriter whom she had known for some time. He came over and kissed her in typically unisex Hollywood fashion.

With that Sean Penn flew into a tantrum and began attacking the songwriter with his fists, his feet, and his chair. Wolinski got away with his life, but he sued for damages. Penn was fined a thousand dollars and was given a year's probation on a jail term for assault and battery.

What was wrong with him?

"The marriage had been undergoing stress at the time," a friend of Madonna's was quoted in Time as saying. "But this was the first major stress, the first really traumatic episode for her. Wolinski was someone she knew, and it really shook her up."

The tantrums did not abate.

Four months later, in August, Penn and Madonna were surrounded by a group of New York paparazzi outside the apartment they were living in on Central Park West. In the argument that ensued after Penn told them all to beat it, one of the photographers, Anthony Savignano, wound up dripping with saliva spat on him by the annoyed and frothing Sean Penn.

Angrily Savignano shoved back at Penn. Penn then unlimbered a right and smashed him. He continued swinging his fists to target one of the other paparazzi, Vinnie Zuffante.

No charges were filed that time.

The upshot of this episode was that Madonna spent less and less of her time with her hair trigger-tempered husband at close range.

Madonna's great-aunt, Elsie Fortin, of Bay City, Michigan, had a few words to tell the press about her niece's marriage.

"It didn't seem like they got along," she said with remarkable understatement. "If you can't get along, why prolong the agony?" It was Aunt Elsie's assessment that the couple's basic problem lay within the psyche of Sean Penn. "I'd say Penn was insanely jealous of her," she said.

As if her marriage problems weren't enough, Madonna now discovered that she had not quite shaken off the bad luck that pursued her film career.

Shanghai Surprise opened to totally devastating reviews:

Chicago Tribune: "*Shanghai Surprise*, a soggy romantic adventure that stars Sean Penn and Madonna, proves that the making of a simple star vehicle now numbers among the lost arts of the cinema. . . . The makers of *Shanghai Surprise*—director Jim Goddard and screenwriters John Kohn and Robert Bentley—seem almost to take a perverse pleasure in preventing their stars from doing anything like what they do best."

Los Angeles Times: " 'Guns cause pain. Opium eases pain,' says Madonna, the bobby-soxed missionary of *Shanghai Surprise*. But even better than opium for avoiding pain is avoiding *Shanghai Surprise* itself, a movie of jaw-dropping, high-water mark dreadfulness."

Financial Times: "This is one of those movies that have the word 'romp' written all through them like a stick of seaside rock. The more you bite into it, the less the word will go away, however sticky and distorted it becomes en route.

First of all, *Financial Times* said, one gets a vicarious frisson of pleasure watching two famous people honeymoon on film. And there is the Shanghai nightlife, the gambling, the restaurants, to focus on. But does this make for a motion picture frolic? Unhappily, no.

"But the direction by Britain's Jim Goddard (late of Parker) turns it all into a rickshaw ride through clichés. Pantomime villains reel up in the dark and heroines swoon at the touch of a male kiss. And George Harrison's song-studded score is no consolation for the continual wish that Madonna would slough the pious vestments of straight acting and seize a passing microphone to burst into song."

Janet Maslin, of *The New York Times*, wrote that the picture was a "widely publicized washout." "And Madonna looks cute in her costumes, dressed as a missionary in a tight navy-blue dress with little white socks. A less successful fashion plate is Mr. Penn, who plays a necktie salesman and adventurer living in the title city, circa 1938." Penn, she pointed out, ever since his hilarious performance as a stoned surfer in *Fast Times at Ridgemont High*, had been greatly overrated.

Richard Corliss, of *People* magazine, wrote that the picture was no winner, but no atrocity either. He was puzzled why MGM should simply release the picture without trying out any marketing strategy on it. "Madonna seems straitjacketed by her role, and Penn, for once, looks bored. She smiles, he glowers. Neither glows like the incandescent movie stars they can and will be."

Madonna had her own thoughts on the picture and the reason for its failure:

"I'm extremely disappointed with it," she said. "The director didn't have an eye for the big screen and he seemed to be in a bit over his head. The film company wanted to make an action film like *Raiders of the Lost Ark*, but the script was actually a very personal love story.

"Unfortunately it was edited as an adventure movie, and they left out all the stuff that was its saving grace. We wanted it to be an old romantic movie like *African Queen*, and that's what we envisioned when we read the script. It was very hard work doing it, so it's a little upsetting.

"They cut all my major scenes down to nothing, which made me look like an airhead girl without any character who had gone to China just on a whim. I also wanted to do a movie that was completely opposite to *Desperately Seeking Susan*, where I played a character who was very close to my own personality. I needed a role where I could prove to people that I could really act and that I wasn't just being myself."

In general *Shanghai Surprise* proved to be a project that never should have been undertaken in the first place.

14

Ticking People Off

By the time Madonna's third album was released in the summer of 1986, she was, of course, a multimillionairess, an established movie star (even with that disaster *Shanghai Surprise* on the big screen at the moment giving the lie to that assessment), and a legend in her own time.

She now had full approval of any material in her albums, singles, or videos, and on the way it was presented. And, for the first time, she was demanding and getting production credit, sharing it on album number three with a record producer named Patrick Leonard, who was the musical director of her 1985 tour, and her old friend from Ann Arbor, Steve Bray.

Leonard was impressed by Madonna's stick-to-itiveness. "She was around for every note," he observed. "She doesn't like musical rules and her instincts just turn the songs into 'Madonna' records." He meant it not as a criticism but as a compliment.

"I like to have control, but I'm not a tyrant," Madonna said. "I like to be surrounded by really talented, intelligent people whom I trust, and ask them for their advice and get their input too."

There was a lot of "family" in album number three. First of all, it was dedicated to Sean Penn, "the coolest guy in the universe." The leadoff song, a number titled "Live to Tell," was featured as the theme for the Sean Penn motion picture *At Close Range*, which he made directly after *Shanghai Surprise*.

Madonna chose the title *True Blue* for the album, taking it from a song of that title in the collection. But the real prize in the album—and by far the most controversial song in the entire group—was one titled "Papa, Don't Preach."

To understand and appreciate the effectiveness of Madonna's presentation of the song, you must realize that by 1986 she had once again remodeled herself into a "new" image. The trampy, sexy look was long gone. A more old-fashioned and feminine aspect was taking its place. Her singing was changing too. She was working in a deeper pitch, in a more expressive voice. In one video made for a number in the third album, she wore honey-blond hair and a really demure Depression-era flowered dress.

"I like challenge and controversy," Madonna told Stephen Holden of *The New York Times* in a story published before the release of the album. "I like to tick people off." Holden noted her "almost demure . . . pink-and-blue flowered dress and a very short haircut," reminding him of the gamine look of an Audrey Hepburn or a Leslie Caron. All the heavy makeup and the junk jewelry—featured elements of her earlier image—had vanished.

Madonna: "After a while I got sick of wearing tons of jewelry. I wanted to clean myself off. I see my new look as very innocent and feminine and unadorned. It makes me feel good. Growing up, I admired the kind of beautiful, glamorous woman—from Brigitte Bardot to Grace Kelly—who doesn't seem to be around much anymore. I think it's time for that kind of glamour to come back."

"Papa, Don't Preach" was the only song in the album that came in from the outside—that is, it was written by Brian Elliot, and not in collaboration with Madonna, Steve Bray, or Patrick Leonard.

"When I first heard the song," Madonna said, "I thought it was silly. But then I thought, wait a minute, this song is really about a girl who is making a decision in her life. She has a very close relationship with her father and wants to maintain that closeness. To me, it's a celebration of life. It says, 'I love you, father, and I love this man and this child that is growing inside me.' Of course who knows how it will end? But at least it starts off positive."

The protagonist of the song, as might be guessed from the description, is a pregnant teenager who begs her father to bless her decision to keep the baby no matter what the consequences. It is sung, according to Holden, "in a passionate, bratty sob that makes the plea immediate and believable."

The video production of the song extended the story line to reinforce the lyrics. To make it ring with authenticity, it was filmed in a working-class neighborhood on Staten Island, with the film star Danny Aiello playing the father. Madonna, of course, was the daughter, looking waifish and saucer-eyed.

Once *True Blue* was released, "Papa, Don't Preach" instantly struck a chord of popularity—and of dissent. The theme of the song—have a baby and let the future take care of itself—annoyed even liberal feminists like columnist Ellen Goodman.

After describing the video and the lyrics of the song, she wrote, "My own personal fantasy is to see just one movie in which the passionate male lead looks deeply into the eyes of the exquisite female lead as they sit before the fire in the lonely cabin, kissing soulfully, and asks whether they should use his contraceptive, or hers. Just once I would like to hear a rock-and-roll song in which the lead singer pants huskily, 'No, no, no.' "

But then, sadly: "Responsible romance is an oxymoron. True lovers are not planners; they are carried away. Just ask pregnant teenagers, almost a million of them a year."

On the flip side of the coin, responsible magazines like *Newsweek* now began to treat Madonna with some artistic respect. Cathleen McGuigan wrote, "Whatever the outcome of her movie career, Madonna is undeniably arresting on camera. Her iconographic glamour shines through more than ever now that she has cropped and bleached her hair and given up wearing heavy chains and crucifixes.

"In her compelling new 'Papa, Don't Preach' video, directed by Peter Percher and with Danny Aiello playing her father, Madonna, in striped T-shirt and jeans, is an insouciant waif. Intercut with the narrative are shots of a trim but voluptuous Madonna singing the song and dancing in a studio. White-throated, red-mouthed, platinum hair swept back, she is a riveting Marilyn Monroe–like presence, without the quivering lip and self-doubt.''

Even the *Christian Science Monitor* took a serious look at the moral point of the controversial song:

Tim Riley noted that the most important number on the album was ''Papa, Don't Preach,'' which was a serious attempt at using music to focus on the controversial subjects of pregnancy and abortion.

Although the number is a dance number, its lyrics blatantly play against happiness to deal conflictedly with a crisis in a young woman's life—a pregnant teener who wants to have and keep her illegitimate child.

''Though the girl's line of reasoning must seem all mixed up to the 'pro-life' and 'pro-choice' lobbies,'' wrote Riley, ''the centerpiece of the song isn't so much its 'message' as the catchy tune set in motion by the little drama conjured up in the lyrics.''

And immediately the activist ''lobbies'' mentioned by Riley were heard from. Alfred Moran, the executive director of Planned Parenthood of New York City, said, ''The message is that getting pregnant is cool and having the baby is the right thing and a good thing and don't listen to your parents, the school, anybody who tells you otherwise—don't preach to me, Papa. The reality is that what Madonna is suggesting to teenagers is a path to permanent poverty.''

But the ''pro-lifers'' disagreed. ''Abortion is readily available on every street corner for young women,'' said Susan Carpenter-McMillan, president of the California chapter of Feminists for Life in America. ''Now what Madonna is telling them is, Hey, there's an alternative.''

A campaign to discourage teenage pregnancy by the Mayor's Office of Adolescent Pregnancy and Parenting Services in New York, coordinated by Alice Radosh, was just beginning, using subway posters, television and radio spots, and carrying the slogan, Be Smart About Sex.

"We're using the same medium to put across a very different message about being smart and avoiding teenage pregnancy," Radosh said. "The timing of the Madonna song concerns us."

By now even *The Washington Post* was inspired to treat Madonna as a full-fledged artist, pointing that the production values of the album were not particularly exceptional.

J. D. Considine first of all expressed disapproval of the lyrics of a Madonna song that went "Oop Shoo Doop Oop Oop Sha La La," pointing out that certainly no one could be expected to do much with those words, not even Madonna. An attack followed on a number of clichés in the lyrics of songs she had composed with Steve Bray and Patrick Leonard, in particular, "Come on, Make My Day," "Love Makes the World Go Round," "Why Do Fools Fall In Love?" and the world-class candidate for tiredest of all: "Baby, I Love You."

The reviewer then went on to point out the many shortcomings of the backup tracks, noting that unlike Tony Thompson's spirited drumming for "Like a Virgin," "the percussion here is mechanically predictable." Considine likewise inveighed against the "sorry salsa" of "La Isla Bonita" and the "freeze-dried disco" of "Where's the Party?"

"Live to Tell" was more than all right— "an exquisite ballad that finds the singer working strictly from strengths." Her "tendency to favor the darker sonorities of her lower register seems far more appropriate, supplying the song with the sort of regret expected of someone baring a secret" that would "burn inside" her. Considine approved of Madonna's dramatic role here that was "quite a way from the superficiality of the rest of the album."

As for the success or failure of the album, it was obviously and definitely a success. In the long run *True Blue* racked up sales of seventeen million worldwide. Number Two, *Like a Virgin*, had sold eleven million, over and against *Madonna*, Number One, which had racked up a total of nine million sales.

Indeed, it took "Papa, Don't Preach," the controversial number in the album, only eight weeks to hit the top—exactly the same way as one of Madonna's other Number One hits, "Like a Virgin," did, with "Virgin" zapping the charts and hitting the top in an incredible five weeks.

Madonna thought her overall success was due to the sudden emergence of the Wannabees.

"What kids see in me is another rebel kid who says what she wants and does what she wants and has a joy in life. The girls that dressed like me all got the joke—it was their parents who didn't. You didn't see those girls going off and doing awful things because they bought my records. What I've learned from all the controversy is that you can't expect everyone to [understand] your sense of humor. But I've also learned that people eventually do catch on to what they don't get at first. It's a nice surprise in the end when they go, 'Hey, well, you know . . . I like that.' "

Her rebellion, she knew, came from the inner conflicts of her early years, which had shaped her and crafted her into an upstart and iconoclast, if indeed she could really be called that.

"When you go to Catholic school," she said, "you have to wear uniforms, and everything is decided for you. Since you have no choice but to wear your uniform, you go out of your way to do things that are different in order to stand out.

"All that rebellion carried over when I moved to New York . . . to became a dancer. At dance classes all the ballerinas had their hair back in a bun, and so I chopped my hair off and ripped my leotard down the front and put little tiny safety pins all the way up just to provoke my teacher. After all, where is it written that in order to be a better dancer you have to wear a black leotard and pink tights and have your hair in a bun?

"Going out dancing with my girlfriends in New York clubs, we would dress for provocation. What I was wearing at the time I was signed to a record contract became my look [on the album cover]."

Besides, Madonna had somehow felt that she would be a success.

"I always thought of myself as a star," she mused, "though I never in my wildest dreams expected to become *this* big. But I knew I was born to it. I don't know why. I think people are named names for certain reasons, and I feel that I was given a special name for a reason. In a way, maybe I wanted to live up to my name."

15

The Search for Madonna's Persona

On paper the screen story looked pretty good. First of all, it was a deliberate attempt at a Golden Age "screwball" comedy, the kind of film exemplified by *It Happened One Night* and later on by a long string of hits, including *The Awful Truth* and *Bringing Up Baby*, in which "baby" turned out to be a young tiger.

Its basic concept was good outrageous farce. Consider the premise: The protagonist is a young, innocent, laid-back yuppie named Loudon Trott, who is about to marry into big bucks. His fiancée is Wendy Worthington, and she's practically unattainable—except for lucky Loudon.

Just prior to the wedding, Wendy's father, Simon Worthington, decides to set a pair of tasks for his young son-in-law-to-be, not realizing, apparently, that they are about as impossible of accomplishment as the labors of Hercules.

NUMBER ONE: Worthington wants Trott to meet a just-released female convict who has been serving a jail sentence (unjustifiably) as a murderess, to send her down to her home in Philadelphia. She's Nikki Finn.

NUMBER TWO: Worthington wants Trott to pick up a rare

cougar for delivery to one of the rich man's clients in mid-Manhattan.

Of course it is obvious to anyone in the audience that the paroled murderess is going to be hard to handle. But Trott doesn't seem to mind. And so he goes blithely off to pick her up at the prison to carry out his father-in-law-to-be's orders.

What happens is that a pair of homicide detectives is trying to track her to London for reasons of their own. Also, a pair of mobsters becomes involved in Nikki's future, too.

Presented with these elements in a script by Andrew Smith and Ken Finkelman, Madonna felt that the whole concept would fly. Smith was the author of the motion picture *The Main Event*, a moderately successful 1979 film starring Barbra Streisand and Ryan O'Neal. It had lots of yelling and screaming in it, but seemed reasonably farcical. Finkelman wrote *Airplane II* and *Grease II*—directing *Airplane II*, with Lloyd Bridges, Peter Graves, William Shatner, and Chad Everett, and scripting *Grease II*, which featured Michelle Pfeiffer, Maxwell Caulfield, Eve Arden, Sid Caesar, Tab Hunter, and Dody Goodman.

What Madonna saw in the role of Nikki Finn was a kind of lovable Judy Holliday, in a reprise of the role she played in *Born Yesterday*.

"Judy Holliday could really come off as being dumb, but she knew exactly what was going on," Madonna said. "I just love those films where the woman gets away with murder but her weapon is laughter, and you end up falling in love with her."

As for the character she would play: "I had a lot in common with Nikki. She's courageous and sweet and funny and misjudged. But she clears her name in the end, and that's always good to do. I'm continuously doing that with the public."

In fact, it was director James Foley, one of the Penn family's best friends (he had worked with Madonna before on video and with Sean on *At Close Range*), who introduced her to the script.

"He knew that I'd wanted to do comedy for a long time, so it was like my reward. There was just something about the character, the contrasts in her nature, how she was tough on one side and vulnerable on the other—that I thought I could take and make my own."

Even with the fiasco of *Shanghai Surprise* hulking in the background, Madonna was still a bankable star, and so she was signed for the picture.

During filming, Madonna spent most of her time on the film set, while her husband Sean spent most of his time at their new opulent Malibu beach house. That instantly fueled rumors in the press that the two were going to split up—or had already split up.

Making that third picture was hard work for Madonna. What was even worse, it all came to nothing when the picture was released. One hint that something was out of kilter came when Warner Bros. refused to allow the film to be screened for review.

All expectations were much higher than the final reception of the film. Vincent Canby reported that on the night the film was premiered in New York's Times Square, at least ten thousand people were crowding into the streets to watch for Madonna and other stars of the film.

The next day at noon Canby arrived at the theater to review the picture at its first regularly scheduled performance in the 1,151-seat Ziegfeld Theater, to find only about sixty people in the house.

"In this age of electronically enhanced personality," he wrote, "fame may be fleeting, but it doesn't disappear overnight." He went on, "Madonna was as big an attraction on Friday at noon as she had been on Thursday evening, but, apparently, her stardom on records, in music videos, in concert, and as a free show in Times Square is not, as they say, translating to the box office of movie theaters."

Variety wrote that *Who's That Girl?* was "a loser."

Michael Wilmington, of the *Los Angeles Times*, equated Madonna's *Who's That Girl?* with earlier screwball comedies of the 1930s, specifically citing Howard Hawks's unbelievably good *Bringing Up Baby*. He pointed out, however, that all the things—including Katharine Hepburn and Cary Grant—that gave the 1938 grace and balance were missing from the Madonna film.

"This movie," he wrote, "wobbles and jerks like a broken gyroscope."

Nor did he like the jokes or the attempt made by the cast to effect a buoyancy that seemed always tired and phony. The nonsense was never "lyrical," as it should be to work. The talent seemed always headed in the wrong direction. Instead of building Madonna, the movie actually downgraded her—"the worst thing" such a vehicle could do.

He blamed the trouble on scriptwriters Andrew Smith and Ken Finkelman, but felt that James Foley, the director, had to share equal blame, even though he *was* able to bring out the warmth, beauty, and charm of Madonna in some of her better-staged scenes.

He wrote that the star "has a lot of magic; in her punk-Marilyn Monroe turns, she radiates the devastatingly but lightly parodied sexiness that Elvis Presley and Tina Turner also used."

Wilmington noted that the only magic of the film was confined to the sound track—precisely, to the star's songs. The character she played was nothing more than a phony cliché pop rebel, "weirdly oblivious, dancing around in Pee-Wee Herman sweetie-jerky hops, wreaking unfunny gun-crazy havoc, and haggling in a Philly screech that sounds like a cross between Judy Holliday and Leo Gorcey. "It's a movie," he concluded "where the cougar has all the best lines."

Vincent Canby blamed the fiasco on the film executives who bankrolled Madonna, pointing out that ever since she had first appeared in the public eye three years before there had always been a large amount of hype surrounding her stardom. Her voice, of course, was noticeably small; her expertise in music was not of supremely high caliber; her personality was a curious amalgam of notable celebrities of the past, reinforced by audiovisual technical expertise at the sound console.

Withal, Canby admitted, "she's a knowing, shrewd, pragmatic young woman, a performer of invigorating energy who still looks a lot like Marilyn Monroe, . . . but who has much more in common with the enthusiastic, unembarrassed, comic tartiness of Jean Harlow."

Canby wound up his review by suggesting that before they let Madonna make another film, her movie backers should sit down and really think out her future—first of all by taking a long hard look at the image she creates in her best music videos. "Open Your Heart," Canby wrote, "in a brisk, haiku-like four minutes and twenty-two seconds, presents Madonna as every adolescent boy's wildest, sweetest fantasy." She was a "potent, pocket-sized sex bomb" to Canby. "So far, though, all it does is tick."

Indeed Madonna had no time to brood over the failure of yet another big-screen venture. She was already involved in another world tour—this one, ironically, conceived to "sell" the movie *Who's That Girl?* The tour was a mind-boggling tour de force, if you will. It covered three continents—Asia, Europe, and America—where two million fans in eighteen key cities would be watching her.

Madonna was tired of tours, but she felt she could make this one work with the proper preparation. "I told my manager the only way I would do the tour was if I could make it interesting for myself. Because that was the challenge; being able to make a show interesting in a stadium where it's impersonal. I wanted to make it really personal."

She put herself through a rigorous program of preparation—seventy hours a week, working out the songs with the band, training for the dances. She would put in two hours every day at home in a huge dance studio and gymnasium, using the weights, working on the trampoline, and swimming in the pool. She rode twenty-five miles up and down the Pacific Coast Highway every day on a ten-speed bike and ran up and down the long, winding stairs of Pepperdine University opening out onto the highway.

Just before starting the tour—in Japan—Madonna was on the Johnny Carson show and had to deny that there was anything going wrong between her and Sean. Already stories were circulating and tongues were wagging.

"He isn't as people imagine him to be," she told Carson. "He's quite a shy person by nature. Am I shy? I have to admit I do flirt a lot. Flirting's part of my makeup. I'll flirt with everybody from garbagemen to grandmothers!"

The kickoff of the tour in Japan was inauspicious at best. A typhoon blew away one of the performances and Madonna had to call off the show. Thousands of fans hung around her hotel that night, singing her name and waiting for her to appear. Which she did, promising to sing when the storm ceased.

"There has probably never been a more imaginative or forceful showcase for the feminine sensibility in pop than Madonna's current concert tour," wrote a *Rolling Stone* writer who had accompanied her to Japan. "She is simply the first female entertainer who has ever starred in a show of this scope, a fusion of Broadway-style choreography and post-disco song and dance that tops the standards set by previous live concert firebrands like Prince and Michael Jackson."

Meanwhile, back in the States, Sean Penn was being himself in his own inimitable, scrappy fashion. While filming a new movie, *Colors*—in which he was playing a rookie cop who was the charge of Robert Duvall as senior partner—he took a swing at Jerrie Klein, an extra, for trying to snap a couple of candid shots of the star on the set. Penn was said to have hit Klein in the nose.

This became a legal problem. Penn was on probation for having taken a swing at Madonna's old friend, songwriter David Wolinski. This current action with Klein was a violation of his earlier probation.

For the time being he was safe. The police took no steps.

However, within days he was speeding in Los Angeles and running a red light. The police picked him up for the light violation. Testing him for alcoholic content, they measured him at just over the legal limit. In court the charge was reduced to reckless driving, but this moving violation was *another* infraction of his probation.

The court sentenced Penn to serve sixty days in jail. He eventually did five, but was paroled out of the country to make a movie in West Germany—a television film titled *Judgment in Berlin*, written by his father, Leo Penn. Once he was through in West Germany, he returned to finish up a total of thirty-three days in jail—with time off for good behavior.

However, his treatment in prison suddenly became another media circus: Was he or was he not getting preferential treatment as an actor and husband of Madonna?

"I was never in fear of my life," Penn said later. "I was

in PC—protective custody. I was in a jail with all the big shots—
one person to a cell. Solitary confinement for twenty-four hours.
So afraid, no. But bored, yes. After two weeks of that kind of
boredom, I think I would have preferred some fear.''

He did a lot of reading and writing, he told an interviewer. ''But the greatest bonus was that [my stay in jail] has
made long airplane trips very easy. Twenty hours to Bang-
kok? No problem. Put me on the plane. With a month of solitary, you do learn patience. Will it last? Time will tell.''

Eventually Penn flew to New York to be with his wife,
Madonna, when she interrupted her own tour of the States to
present a special Madison Square Garden concert in memory
of Martin Burgoyne, who had died of AIDS.

In spite of their occasional appearances together, the rumors about the Penns would not die down. Stories surfaced
that Penn had suddenly demanded that Madonna take a test
for AIDS. Rumors circulated that Penn had moved out of their
house in Malibu and then moved back in again. There were
rumors that they were getting a divorce; there were rumors
that they were already divorced.

Gene Siskel, the film critic, asked Penn why he thought
the press was so fascinated with him and his wife.

''I think the problems came about because—and I hope
you understand how I'm using this vulgar expression—I wasn't
a good little nigger actor who remained quiet, made my films
and stayed out of the way of the press.

''Instead, I think I became labeled as the bad little nigger
who married the white girl, a girl who was as white as they
come. She belonged to them, to the public. And if anybody
took her, I think they thought it should have been someone
more acceptable, like Donald Trump.

''The public is very possessive about rock stars, and about
her—Madonna—in particular. They don't want to share their
love.''

Madonna had something to say about the press and the
way it targeted them—especially her husband.

''They bait Sean in ways I can't even tell you,'' she said.
''They call me obscene names in front of him just to get him
to react. How would you react if someone said *that* about your

wife? And that movie extra he hit [in Los Angeles], he wasn't really an extra—he was a paparazzi *posing* as an extra. You'd have to be a pacifist or a Buddhist to be able to handle it.

"But Sean is trying to learn not to take the bait, and I think he will emerge . . . as a better person and as an even greater actor."

Nevertheless, "We're separated all the time, and that doesn't make it any better. We are a Hollywood couple, so people are going to pay a lot of attention to our marriage. If we have fights, I think that's pretty normal for young people in their first few years of marriage, especially when you have to put up with all the pressures we've been under. I think the fact that we're still together is pretty amazing. You know, we're working it out. It's easy to give up, but it's not easy for me to give up."

Her "Who's That Girl?" tour was getting mixed reviews, but most of them were positive, at least to some degree.

"I've seen the Springsteen stadium tour, I've seen Dylan and the [Grateful] Dead, and I was at Live Aid. Out of all those shows, Madonna's is the only one I'd want to see again," said J. D. Considine, of the *Baltimore Sun*, in an interview. "You need a larger-than-life show if you want to come off in a stadium, and Madonna does. She's not that large physically, but she holds your attention, just as Michael Jackson did in the best of the 'Victory' tours."

Anne Ayers, assistant entertainment editor of *USA Today*, saw her differently: "She's going for a certain kind of show: a Broadway, show-biz, song-and-dance spectacle. In that context it's hard to make a connection with the audience, and I'd have to say she didn't."

"I've heard the talk about how Madonna can't sing, and I can tell you that's bull," said Patrick Leonard, the tour's bandleader who had cowritten much of the *True Blue* album. "She's a natural, intuitive singer with great intonation; she puts across a vulnerable quality that you can't copy, and I know, because I've heard people try."

"She's a natural comedienne and has no trouble laughing at herself," wrote the *Christian Science Monitor*'s Amy Duncan. "One gets the feeling she can change her look with impunity, because her personal charisma and stage presence remain intact." As for her voice, "What has changed somewhat [from the time she started] is the voice, which is darker and richer than it was on the first album."

In August Madonna played to over a quarter of a million people in Britain, and then crossed the English Channel to France. And there, in Paris, disaster almost struck.

Madonna's concert was scheduled for Sceaux Park, a famous seventeenth-century landmark located in a tiny community south of Paris. Complete with manicured trees, splendid lawn, and rare orangery, Sceaux was designed by André Lenôtre, responsible for Paris's Tuileries Gardens as well as the famous gardens at the Palace of Versailles.

When Pierre Ringenbach, the mayor of Sceaux, heard of the plans for the Madonna concert in his select park, he simply canceled the concert. But that was not the end of the story. Madonna had her own special fans in Paris.

One of them was Claude Chirac, the twenty-four-year-old daughter of Jacques Chirac, France's prime minister. Interestingly enough, in a political overlap, the prime minister is also the mayor of Paris.

Claude began her campaign in typically American fashion—a ploy that could only annoy any true Frenchman. She played Madonna videos everywhere, played her songs to everyone she could, caused articles to appear in the papers.

"Like many young people," she said in an interview with Agence-France Press, "I love [Madonna]. I thought it would be bad to be deprived of such a great artist."

Finally she made her father listen to Madonna on record. When the prime minister finally bowed to his daughter's inflexible determination, he approached the Administrative Council of Hauts-de-Seine, where Sceaux is located, to try to overrule the mayor. The park actually *belongs* to Hauts-de-Seine, not the town of Sceaux.

The mayor of Sceaux blew up. "Why in the world is the prime minister interested in a spectacle like this?" he shouted. "I don't know very much about Madonna, but I know the park is not the proper place for a concert like that! I've read some of the articles about Madonna, and I'm not very impressed with her."

Nevertheless Chirac persuaded the Administrative Council of Hauts-de-Seine to overrule the mayor. Interviewed by *Podium*, one of France's leading teenage magazines, Chirac explained why he worked so hard for Madonna.

"This is a great and beautiful artist. She is superb." He pointed out that another reason for his intercession in the affair was the fact that "the immense majority of young people [in France] cannot attend concerts abroad."

In addition to all his help, the prime minister autographed fifty concert tickets for the teenagers' magazine to distribute, and invited Madonna to City Hall.

Visiting Paris City Hall on August 28, Madonna was presented with a five-hundred-thousand-franc donation—about eighty-five thousand dollars—to French charities for AIDS.

"Everybody likes you very, very much," Chirac said to Madonna in English.

"I like you too," Madonna responded, also in English.

Chirac hugged her for a picture. The caption under the photo in the Paris tabloid *Liberation* read, "Who's that girl at the side of the gentleman?"

The "Who's That Girl?" concert was performed on August 29 as scheduled to about 130,000 at Sceaux Park. The attendance, it was noted, was the largest ever for a rock concert in France.

After all the dust had settled and the concert was deemed a success, the press noted that the prime minister's reason for interceding in the Madonna affair was a simple one: to try to gain political advantage over his opponents in the tough upcoming 1988 election. He was playing for support from young French voters.

"I thought Mr. Chirac only liked military music," Jack Lang, the former minister of culture, observed pointedly in an interview.

The Socialist newspaper *Le Matin* began a story, "Santa Madonna, Jacques Chirac has discovered rock 'n' roll."

At the end of the long, exhausting three-continent tour, Madonna declared she would put a temporary halt to making records. She wanted, she said, to concentrate on theatrical work rather than music. She was even considering setting up her own production company, Siren Films.

"After the 'Who's That Girl?' tour I said to myself that I didn't want to hear any of my songs again," Madonna observed. "I didn't know whether I'd ever write another one. I returned [home] feeling so burned out I was convinced I wouldn't go near music for quite a while."

But then—

"Pat Leonard built this new studio, and I went to see it. Within an hour, we'd written this great song. It *amazed* me."

Nevertheless her next ventures tended to be theatrical in general rather than musical.

16

"I WAS MARRIED ONCE"

Madonna's personal life took a nosedive Thanksgiving week, 1987. Because of her tight work schedule and because of her husband's burgeoning film career, the two Penns saw each other more off than on during the bulk of the year. However, they seemed to have been able to accommodate each other by making small sacrifices here and there.

By the time the end of the year was rolling around, it was a different story. Madonna was working in New York, and Penn was around and about. Although Thanksgiving was a family occasion, Penn did not show up at the apartment during the days preceding the holiday.

Then, suddenly and surprisingly, he appeared on Thanksgiving and told Madonna he was expecting a Thanksgiving dinner with all the trimmings. Madonna quickly shot back at him: "You're not having Thanksgiving dinner here!"

At least that was the story as it appeared in the New York *Daily News*. The Liz Smith story said that Madonna was reportedly angered by Penn because he went four days without talking to her and then turned up at their New York home expecting to spend Thanksgiving with her.

"Not so," retorted Madonna, or words to that effect. She insisted that it was not the Thanksgiving events that caused the rift at all.

"There was no direct incident leading up to this," Madonna's publicist, Liz Rosenberg, explained. "It was a series of cumulative pressures. There were many moments in their marriage when it was shaky, and Madonna was finally forced to face the reality of the situation—that they weren't happy together."

Even though Liz Smith's story hinted that the divorce papers had already been filed, they were not really officially filed until after a discussion between Madonna and her attorney the week following Thanksgiving.

As for Penn, he spoke through his own press agent, Lois Smith: "The decision [to divorce] was mutual." The story about Penn's disappearance for four days and then his sudden reappearance was "nonsense," in Lois Smith's words.

Through Rosenberg, Madonna made her attitude about the situation known to the public. "She wanted the marriage to work," Rosenberg said. "All the jokes about the marriage motivated her to work hard at making the marriage go. I don't think she considered him [Penn] in terms of her career."

Penn's press agent said, "I know the tendency in these matters is to always blame [the man], but it is really too bad because these two people love each other."

On Wednesday after Thanksgiving Penn went over to the Columbus Café, a place where he and Madonna had frequented in the past and were well known, and told friends that divorce papers had been served on him. He said he was going back to the West Coast.

Accordingly he left the Manhattan apartment the next day. Madonna spent Thanksgiving at her sister's home in Brooklyn.

What *really* happened during those days was specifically—nothing. In fact, even the divorce papers were not filed until December 4. The papers themselves cited "irreconcilable differences" in the sometimes turbulent, sometimes quiescent, and almost always conflicted marriage.

When the newspaper story of the divorce broke, the paparazzi were alerted, and almost at once journalists were trying to spot either of the Penns for pictures and questions.

One comic bit occurred when Madonna's brother, Christopher Ciccone, stayed at her apartment one night in Manhattan. The paparazzi waiting outside with binoculars suddenly got out their cameras and tried to take pictures of what they assumed was a new boyfriend.

Madonna flew to Los Angeles to file the papers after eluding the journalists, but then she apparently had second thoughts, for on December 17, two weeks later, she showed up at the Santa Monica Superior Court and filed a petition to *dismiss* her request for divorce!

"Madonna's request for dismissal of her divorce action was granted Wednesday in Domestic Relations Court," the *Chicago Tribune* said on December 18. The document asked that the divorce petition be dismissed "without prejudice"—legalese adopted to keep open the option to go ahead with the divorce if the petitioner decided later on to revert to her original wish.

Meanwhile Penn had also moved back to Los Angeles, where he was scheduled to start shooting another film.

"He's not very happy," said his press agent. "It's not a very happy experience having your marriage break up, and it's very difficult when you have to do it in front of the world. He feels terrible."

Sometime after Thanksgiving Penn was in Los Angeles, at a place called Helena's, an exclusive late-night club. There he proceeded to have a few drinks and indulge in a little self-pity. To his rather glazed-over shock, he recognized Vincent Zuffante, the photographer he had decked a year before, having a drink with singer Billy Idol.

Penn called in Helena, the owner, and persuaded her to toss Zuffante out on his ear. Helena, knowing Penn's reputation, talked Zuffante into leaving, even though Zuffante pointed out quite logically and correctly that he didn't even have his camera with him!

Later on, according to *Time* magazine, when Penn got up to go to the men's room, he discovered to his chagrin that there was a long waiting line. He headed outside to relieve himself against the side of the building.

In September Madonna had seen a motion picture titled *House of Games*, written and directed by David Mamet, a Broadway playwright who had won a 1984 Pulitzer Prize for his play *Glengarry Glen Ross*. Later he had done the screenplay for the motion picture *The Untouchables*, based on the television series of the same name that played between October 1959 and September 1963 starring Robert Stack—the story about Eliot Ness of the FBI and his battle with the Al Capone gang. *House of Games* was a story about a female psychiatrist and best-selling author who becomes involved with a con man and his team of sharp operators. A Hitchcockian tale, it was told with charm and verve.

Madonna was sufficiently impressed to write a letter of praise to Mamet. "It was the first movie I had seen in a long time that had stimulating language," she said. "I didn't feel it had been written for the masses. So I wrote my first fan letter."

She never heard from Mamet, but he read her letter.

When she saw a notice in the trades about the casting of a short play by David Mamet with the unlikely title of *Speed-the-Plow*, she immediately contacted the director, Gregory Mosher, through Mike Nichols, whom Madonna had met. She and Penn had previously worked with Mosher in a workshop production of David Rabe's play *Goose and Tom-Tom*—done for the Lincoln Center workshop; in *Goose* she had played a gangster's moll. No one ever heard of it because the press was banned from the production and it received no attention.

Mosher knew who she was and remembered her, of course, and invited her to an audition for the part. One audition was not quite enough. Mosher invited her back for a second. During these lengthy run-throughs, Mosher jotted down notes for "small but significant rewrites" to accommodate the part for her. He then contacted Mamet, and the rewrites were made.

In the end Mosher hired her. "Madonna brings [to the role] a backbone of steel," he said. "Mamet made the character, rather than a poor soul who is battered to the ground, someone about whom there is an element of doubt."

The key question of the play's motivation involves the true

nature of her character; is it real, or feigned?

"The audience is meant to go out asking one another, Is she an angel? Is she a whore?"

The meaning of the title, *Speed-the-Plow*, is somewhat ambiguous. It is apparently derived from an old-fashioned blessing found in medieval verse and song, which goes, "God speed your plow." What it seems to mean is "Do your work, and God will help you."

Mosher added one important extra subtext: "It has to do with turning fresh earth—and of course there is a sexual pun."

The three-character play turns on two men, played by Joe Mantegna and Ron Silver, and a woman, played by Madonna. It is set in Hollywood, and concerns the making of films. The two men, who head the production department of a movie studio, are both cynical manipulators, though one is not quite so cynical as the other. The woman is an office temporary, hired to fill in for the regular secretary, who is ill.

Of the two producers, Bobby Gould (Mantegna) is the less cynical and Charlie Fox (Silver) the more. Bobby bets Charlie five hundred dollars that he (Bobby) can seduce the temporary, known only as Karen. He gives her a book that has been sent in for consideration but has already been deemed unproduceable as a movie property and asks her to read it and report on it to him at his home.

The book is titled *The Bridge: Or Radiation and the Half Life of Society. A Study in Decay.* It is a book about the death of civilization.

Karen likes it. She pitches it to Bobby at his home. Certain that it is a work of genius, she reads parts to him, speaks of purity and the need for courage, and of beauty and decency and so on. Bobby is touched and decides to make the film.

But Charlie, enraged that Bobby has momentarily renounced cynicism, destroys the girl verbally and throws her out. In so doing, he gains control of the team, reestablishing cynicism and sophistication at the expense of truth and decency—and leaves Bobby destroyed, too, a man who has blown his one chance to do something good in his life.

The trick in the play is to leave the audience unsure whether the book that is the center of the controversy is really good or really bad and whether the temporary played by Madonna is actually intelligent and on the right track or a dummy who doesn't know art from trash.

To play the role, Madonna darkened her hair, almost back to its natural shade, and costumed herself with a sense of female propriety directly opposite to her usual style. In delivering her lines, she altered her style, too, speaking in grave, restrained tones with not one particle of teen defiance. She even wore glasses sometimes.

It was a risky piece of business, in a professional sense, for her to place herself between two flawless character actors cast in scene-chewing roles, yet she took the chance.

As she worked on the role to shape it into what she wanted—and what the writer and director wanted—she learned a great deal about stagecraft. And those working with her learned a great deal about her too.

"She's mesmerizing," Mosher said about her. He knew she had appeared on the stage only as a gun moll in the 1986 workshop production of *Goose and Tom-Tom*. He knew that she would attract a great deal of attention from the press because of her name. They would be waiting to cream her no matter how she performed.

Joe Mantegna was impressed by her professionalism. He knew she was not the first choice for the part, yet he approved of the way she pitched into the production once she got started.

"Madonna didn't Bogart her way into the role," he said. "A lot of high-powered actresses also auditioned."

Mosher was happy with her manner of working. "In six weeks of rehearsals, there hasn't been one mucky moment," he said as they approached opening night.

Ron Silver added, "She's funny, feisty, and the first one to know her lines."

Mantegna seconded that. "This girl does not lack confidence." Interestingly enough, Mantegna knew both Madonna and Sean Penn personally. He realized they were having problems with their marriage at the time. "They're just people stuck in a position that's very trying," he said. "It's not like I have to have two guys"—he meant bodyguards—"walking next to me all the time," the way Penn did.

As for Madonna, even with all the hard work and her

own confidence that she was a good actress, she knew that she would be pilloried by the critics when the show opened. And because her marriage was beginning to come apart at the seams and the public was aware of it, she knew the press would be waiting to seize upon everything there was to criticize about her.

Why, then, did she take the part and give the media such a good shot at her?

"I've become much more tolerant of people and human error," she said. "Being constantly scrutinized and criticized as I am, you simply have to become tolerant—and a bit passive."

Madonna? Passive?

She was right, of course. The critics *were* waiting for her, circling the theater like killer sharks.

"Being vacant on the stage requires more effort than it does in real life," Howard Kissell wrote in the New York *Daily News*. "Elegantly designed, impeccably directed, *Speed-the-Plow* is Mamet's clearest, wittiest play. I bet it would be even funnier with an actress."

The headlines above all that read, NO, SHE CAN'T ACT.

Frank Rich of *The New York Times* praised her "intelligent, scrupulously disciplined comic acting." This in turn inspired Dennis Cunningham of WCBS-TV to respond, "I'm so ticked off. . . . I think Frank [Rich] should apologize for every actor he's ever given a bad review to."

New York magazine critic John Simon was appalled at Cunningham's antics. "I'm not a historian, but to my knowledge, [in the past] critics have not gone into the public media and attacked one another." About Madonna, Simon said, "She does not literally fall on her fanny, but not a hell of a lot of work has gone into the performance."

Michael Kuchwara, of the Associated Press, wrote of Madonna, "Absolutely on target, demolishing the egomaniacs who decide what reaches the silver screen."

David Richards analyzed Madonna's performance for *The Washington Post*: "That Karen is all but blown into the woodwork is as inevitable as *Jaws II* or *Friday the 13th, Part 9*. Still, Mamet gives her more of a fighting chance than is apparent in Madonna's performance. A potential three-way clash has been reduced to the head-on collision of two hungry men, and the possibilities for misunderstanding and manipulation are correspondingly diminished.

"Can Madonna act? No, not particularly well. . . . But she doesn't do irreparable damage to the play. . . . Her name will sell tickets and help focus attention on a play that merits wide exposure."

Time: "It's not a big part, but Madonna is solid, line-perfect; she holds you. You're surprised. The people who put Madonna in the show are not. Mamet and director Gregory Mosher say they were sure of her after her first audition."

Madonna talked freely to *Vanity Fair*'s Kevin Sessums about her Broadway experience with Mamet and Mosher.

"It was a real mind-fuck of a script," she said frankly. "Brilliant, but confusing. My part ended up being a plot manipulation. But at first I saw her [the character Karen] as an angel of mercy who was coming down to save everybody."

But that was apparently not the full truth.

"Little did I know," Madonna continued, "that David Mamet and Greg Mosher and everybody else involved saw me as a vixen, a dark, evil spirit. That didn't dawn on me till halfway through rehearsals, when David kept changing my lines to make me more and more a bitch, a ruthless, conniving little witch.

"So, in the middle of this process I was devastated that my idea of the character wasn't what she was at all. That was a really upsetting experience. It was like getting trampled on every night. Mamet is a stubborn man—he is not interested in collaborating. . . . I think he's interested in fascism."

"A Mussolini with a sense of meter?" suggested Sessums.

"Precisely. But he's a charming man," Madonna admitted.

So much for the ambiguous interpretations of the female character in the three-character plot that seemed to many to be a catalyst to the interior character conflicts of the two male protagonists.

A final statement about Madonna's acting by Billy Hopkins, the casting director on *Desperately Seeking Susan* and, co-incidentally, on *Speed-the-Plow:* "I don't think she's a great actress. But she has something that enabled her to stay in the forefront of people's minds for six, seven years. . . . She . . . has something that nobody else has, and is smart enough to recognize it and utilize it. She's got street smarts."

But street smarts were not enough to enable her to hold her marriage together. For over a full year now Madonna had been struggling desperately to strengthen her relationship with Sean Penn. Even in the first months of their marriage insecurities had infiltrated the liaison. There were so many differences in their personalities—along with so many similarities—that trouble seemed continually on the brink of eruption.

"The singer always had trouble with Sean's unpredictable outbursts," *Time* magazine reported in December 1987, "and [Madonna] sought psychiatric help for herself soon after the wedding."

Accordingly, some of her friends tried to get her to persuade her husband to seek similar professional help. Whether or not he did so is unknown. Later on, of course, he was forced into therapy by court order.

Another problem rose. A number of Madonna's close friends did not like Penn and were unable to get along with him. They viewed him as immature and spoiled and were likewise appalled by his excessive drinking and his tiny-tot temper tantrums.

Even Penn's own circle understood some of the problems and sympathized with Madonna. "Sean has a lot of insecurities," one friend said.

Madonna admitted the same thing: "I have my insecure moments, and that puts a lot of strain on people. You take things out on the person you love, and that causes fights, alienation, grief, shrink sessions, and a lot of ca-ca."

"The divorce is not all his fault," said one of Penn's associates.

During 1988 there was an incident that took place in the lives of Madonna and Sean Penn that reached the press in distorted or unconfirmed form. That effusion was called a "night of terror" by the press and portrayed a number of actions that allegedly took place in the Malibu home of the Penns.

There was an exaggerated picture of the domestic life of the Penns drawn by the journalist who wrote the story, including several incidents that eventually ended up in an altercation between Sean and Madonna.

Apparently someone called the police and soon the house was surrounded. Madonna must have escaped the crowd, for she appeared later on in the sheriff's office with her story. Sean Penn then accused Madonna of making it all up. Madonna charged the *press* with inventing the story.

However, it was on that same night—December 28, 1988— that she filed for divorce action for the second time.

She refused to discuss the details of her tempestuous affair with the press. "People want to hear the dirt, but this is not really anything I want to talk about. . . . It's totally unfair to Sean. I have great respect for him. It's like most relationships that fail. It's not one thing. It's many things that go on over a period of time. It's been a slow breaking point all the way."

In 1991 she told *Vanity Fair*, "Sean was very protective of me. He was like my father in a way. He patrolled what I wore."

SEAN: You're not wearing *that* dress. You can see everything in that.

"At least he was paying attention to me," she pointed out. "At least he had the balls. And I liked his public demonstrations of protecting me. In retrospect I understand why he dealt with the press the way he did, but you have to realize it's a losing battle. It's not going to get you anywhere, and I don't think Sean can give that up. He'll defend you to the death—it's irrational, but also noble."

About the breakup of her marriage Madonna was definitely conflicted. As a Catholic she looked back on her divorce as a sacrilege. As a person she knew the relationship could never possibly have worked.

"Sean and I had problems. We had this high-visibility life, and that had a lot to do with the demise of the marriage. When you're always being watched, you almost want to kill each other."

She told Lynn Hirschberg, "I still go to see his movies,

though." She confessed that Penn's latest, *State of Grace*, gave her a strange feeling. The actress Robin Wright played opposite him; the two were then engaged to be married. At the time Wright was pregnant with their child.

Madonna felt "embarrassed" to see it because she knew "everyone's going to see me going into the movie." Anyway, "It's just a movie, they're just acting," she thought. "Until it got to the kissing-nipple scene. And then I was, like, I can't watch this. I am going to throw up. I still feel territorial—it's like, 'Hands off, bitch! I was married to him!' "

But that was all far in the future. During her own period of intense emotional distraction during the breakup of her marriage, Madonna was continuing to appear on Broadway in the Mamet play, which remained on the boards for a nine-month period, a pretty good stretch for a play that might not have lasted anywhere near that long without the drawing power of Madonna in the cast.

By the time the curtain fell for the last time in February 1989, Madonna was free of Sean Penn and free of her dedication to Broadway.

About Broadway she did have something to say in public: "It was just grueling, having to do the same thing every night, playing a character who is so unlike me. I didn't have a glamorous or flamboyant part. I was a scapegoat. That's one of the things that attracted me to [the role]. Still, night after night, that character failed in the context of the play. To continue to fail each night and to walk off that stage crying, with my heart wrenched—it just got to me after a while. I was becoming as miserable as the character I played."

She had lost two important things: her illusions about love and marriage and her illusions about acting on the stage.

Her divorce was, as Madonna admitted, the most tragic event, next to her mother's death, in her life. "I went through a period when I felt like a total failure—as any good Catholic girl would. But I'm over it now. I don't feel like a failure anymore. I just feel sad. Every once in a while at night I'll wake up and go, 'My God! I was married once. I was married and he was the love of my life.' It is like a death to deal with. It's very, very difficult."

What she needed was therapy.

For Madonna, therapy equaled work—hard work.

She got together with her old friend Steve Bray and her associate Patrick Leonard and set out to dream up material for a new album.

About what went on between Madonna and Sean Penn, Bray had this to say: "I think it was just two people who were basically incompatible at the end. They tried very, very hard to make their relationship work, but in the end there was something inherently incompatible in their natures."

17

Pepsi-Cola Hits the Spot

Getting back to work turned out to be exactly the right move for Madonna to make in trying to forget her frustrating three years of marriage to Sean Penn. In working with Steve Bray and Patrick Leonard on material for a new album, she found cathartic inspiration in molding her emotional problems in lyrical expressions of love, frustration, and grief.

In a matter of weeks the team found it had enough ideas for an album's worth of songs. The concepts simply poured out once the creative juices started flowing.

"We wrote 'Like a Prayer,' 'Spanish Eyes,' 'Till Death Do Us Part,' 'Dear Jessie,' 'Promise to Try,' and 'Cherish' in a two-week period," Leonard reported.

Madonna worked on the lyrics, reaching into her recent past for emotional inspiration.

She recalled that Leonard would frequently throw her some music he had written and she would listen to it over and over. "And somehow the music suggests words to me and I just start writing words down. Other times I will come to Pat with an idea for a song, either lyrically or emotionally, and say, 'Let's do something like this,' or I'll have a melody line in my head which I will sing to him, and he will sort of pound out the chords. It takes a lot longer to do it that way, because I don't play an instrument, but ultimately it's a lot more personal."

She worked with Steve Bray in a similar fashion. "Sometimes he'll come up with a track, and he'll have a verse and chorus, but he won't have a bridge"—the musical "release" that plays counter to the main melodic figure, usually in a different key, and leads right back to the main figure for final restatement and conclusion—"so we'll write the bridge usually together."

With Bray she worked on "Express Yourself" and "Keep It Together," and a pair of love songs titled "First Is a Kiss" and "Love Attack." The latter two were dropped from the lineup, since they did not seem to conform to the obviously "confessional" mood of the rest of the numbers.

"This was an album she needed to do," Bray said. "I'm sure of it. It was a cathartic kind of thing to do. If she's in love, she'll write love songs. If she's not in love she definitely won't be writing love songs. That's why the love songs we recorded aren't on the LP—she didn't feel that they were real enough for her at the time."

As might be guessed by the title, "Till Death Do Us Part" is a more or less backward look at Madonna's relationship with Sean Penn. Writing the song with Leonard, Madonna pulled no punches. At one point the lyrics reveal bruises from the relationship that were both physical and emotional. When he made demands on her, she refused to obey, and when he began to fight back, she retaliated with a lie. In the end there was no truth, and love was dead.

Ouch!

In the rest of the song Madonna reveals her helplessness under the spell cast by the marriage vows, but she can still feel compassion toward a man who seems to hate himself almost as much as he hates those about him.

In an ingenious mixture of conflicting modes, the somewhat bitter, cruel lyrics play against a danceable, lilting, musical beat.

In "Promise to Try," Madonna addresses her feelings and

thoughts about the loss of her mother when she was a tiny child. In fact Madonna dedicated the album itself to her mother for teaching her "how to pray."

The lyrics expose Madonna's feelings of abandonment and loss and her attempts to live up to the precious memories she still holds of her mother's presence.

"Oh Father" is a rather metaphoric piece in which Madonna explores her paternal instincts. It becomes a somewhat facile study of those instincts as they surface again and again in her life during relationships dominated by male machismo. The effect of the lyrics is frequently ambivalent—cruelty leavened by simpatico. That is, the cruelty inflicted on her may simply be the result of cruelty inflicted on her tormentor in the past.

In "Keep It Together," Madonna explores the emotional stability of a large family, along with the sometime polarization of siblings in the incessant rivalry between individual brothers and sisters.

"Like a Prayer" would become the title song of the album, and the music video for the song would create even more comment—and in the end cause a furor in the advertising and marketing business. It would also embroil a totally innocent outsider in the controversy: the Pepsi-Cola Company!

To begin with, the Pepsi-Cola tie-in was a brilliant marketing ploy. The idea was to unite Madonna's built-in appeal to millions of Americans with an advertising campaign celebrating Pepsi-Cola. With the advertising executives at BBDO already having tested out the sales power of such rock-and-roll stars as Tina Turner, David Bowie, Gloria Estefan, and the Miami Sound Machine, not to mention Michael Jackson, it was time for Madonna's name to come up.

The Madonna deal first surfaced sometime in May 1988, while the singer was involved in her Broadway interlude. Roger Mosconi, a creative director and art director at BBDO, was in the throes of searching out a good ploy to increase the Pepsi-Cola account's advertising spread on an international level. Pepsi was strong in the United States market, but weak overseas—only a distant second to Coca-Cola on a worldwide basis, a fact that had become a burr under the saddle blanket to BBDO's client.

"We wanted to start making a lot of noise," Mosconi said, referring to the creative department at the agency. They were in the midst of developing five potential international spots, and it was then that the idea of going to Madonna was seriously discussed.

Instead of getting her approval first and then having her okay the ideas as they were developed, the agency decided to present her with the ideas already in place. If she liked even one, they would sign her up and go ahead.

Four creative artists, including copywriters Michael Patti and Jonathon Mandell, art director Dan Schneider, and producer Tony Frere, flew to California with Mosconi to meet Madonna at her home. Of the five concepts presented to her, she liked one that featured a tribal aborigine roaming the desert—searching for a drink? The idea was used only peripherally in the teaser of the finished spot. Madonna turned down all the other ideas.

Also, she seemed somewhat reluctant to appear in any commercial at all. She *had* broken ground in the world of television commercials in Japan, when she had made a spot for Mitsubishi. The money from BBDO was tempting, particularly when she was spending so much of her time on Broadway, far away from the epicenter of the music business—where, for her, the big money still lay.

She agreed to deal, in a tentative way. If she didn't like what the team brought her, she wouldn't deal; if she did, she would.

Eventually the team came up with a concept with the working title, "Make a Wish," that involved a touching kind of nostalgia. The idea was that the adult Madonna would be looking back on her youth, via flickering old home movies of her eighth birthday. Then the young and adult Madonnas would exchange places and live in each other's lives—Madonna reprising her teen days in Pontiac, Michigan, and the child looking ahead to Madonna's elegant living room in Malibu.

In addition, the song she had just written, "Like a Prayer," would back up the commercial. This was a new idea, using an advertiser's big money to promote a song in tandem with a drink!

Now the creative team went after a director for the commercial. Madonna thought she would like a film director like Tony Scott or Adrian Lyne. But BBDO favored Joe Pytka. After all, Pytka had done the Michael Jackson commercial for Pepsi-Cola, the success of which had led the team to Madonna.

"[Madonna] didn't want to use a commercial director," Mosconi said. "It helped that Joe [Pytka] had just finished a feature [film]." It was called *Let It Ride.* When Tony Frere showed Madonna Pytka's work for the big screen, she was impressed, and the project got under way with Pytka in place as director.

The shooting of the commercial took an unbelievable ten days to complete—eight with Madonna and two in the desert for the opener with the aborigine. For security reasons production was confined to the closed gates of Culver City Studios. A street scene was built on one stage, a church on another, and Madonna's childhood house on still another. The only location shots other than the desert stuff were taken at a local Catholic school.

During the filming Madonna had suggestions of her own, both serious and not so serious.

"She was very concerned with the shooting of her handling the product," Mosconi said. "She didn't want to put her hand up with a Pepsi can." In the long run, Pepsi's presence throughout the spot was rather subtle, even in the moderately gestured toast the young and adult Madonnas give each other at the end.

For the not-so-serious side, Madonna suggested to Pytka that the story of the commercial involve her and a young man in a short romantic interlude, with the boyfriend packing a Pepsi can in his pants pocket. She would then greet him with a Madonnaesque smile and the words: "Is that a Pepsi in your pocket, or are you just happy to see me?"

Twenty-five thousand feet of film was shot to get the final cut of the two-minute commercial. There were a lot of setups shot for "Make a Wish," including a long dance sequence in a street. There were also significant amounts of footage "that make you select what you won't use instead of what you can't use," as the cutter, Rob Watzke, noted.

Watzke did not start cutting until all the film was shot. "The initial turnaround was pretty quick," he said. "We had our first cut in a day."

Pepsi-Cola was wildly enthusiastic about the commercial when it was completed and trumpeted the concept in a press release:

"The ground-breaking deal is expected to change the way popular tunes from major artists are released in the future. Traditionally, new songs have been made public through heavy radio air-play. In an innovative twist, the Madonna deal uses television to provide unparalleled international exposure for her new single . . . where Madonna takes a special trip back in time to revisit her childhood memories."

It then noted that the music video of "Like a Prayer" would debut on MTV on March 3, with the single released March 7 and the album March 21. One story contained a sentence that proved to be a foreshadowing of unmitigated disaster: "The song video will be different than the Pepsi ad."

Disregarding the fractured grammar, the point is that Pepsi had not *seen* the video at all, nor had it made any *plans* to see it. And "different" the song video certainly was!

"Pepsi is confident the song will be a hit," the release said. The video most decidedly was a hit. A hit out of the ballpark.

Even Mosconi was tipped and should have known something was up.

"One day," he recalled, "Madonna, who liked to joke with me, came up to me and said, 'Hey, Roger, are you going to have the burning cross reflecting in the Pepsi can?' And I said, 'What burning cross?' And she smiled and said, 'You'll see.' "

In short the video of "Like a Prayer" was *totally*, even *shockingly*, different from the commercial. It needs to be seen to feel the impact of the visuals backing up the song's more or less mundane lyrics.

The video included images of interracial love, religious ecstasy, stigmata, and burning crosses backed up with a pop-gospel singing of the lyrics. The video is a heady swirl of sacred and profane images—titillating and sensational all at once.

Madonna explained the plot of the video story line to *The*

New York Times in these words: " 'Like a Prayer' is the song of a passionate young girl so in love with God that it is almost as though He were the male figure in her life. From around eight to twelve years old, I had the same feelings. I really wanted to be a nun."

About the video story she said, "A girl on the street witnesses an assault on a young woman. Afraid to get involved because she might get hurt, she is frozen in fear. A black man walking down the street also sees the incident and decides to help the woman. But just then the police arrive and arrest him. As they take him away, she looks up and sees one of the gang members who assaulted the girl. He gives her a look that says she'll be dead if she tells.

"The girl runs, not knowing where to go until she sees a church. She goes in and sees a saint in a cage, who looks very much like the black man on the street, and says a prayer to help her make the right decision. He seems to be crying but she is not sure.

"She lies down on a pew and falls into a dream in which she begins to tumble in space with no one to break her fall. Suddenly she is caught by a woman who represents earth and emotional strength and who tosses her back up and tells her to do the right thing. Still dreaming, she returns to the saint, and her religious and erotic feelings begin to stir. The saint becomes a man. She picks up a knife and cuts her hands. That's the guilt in Catholicism that if you do something that feels good, you will be punished.

"As the choir sings, she reaches an orgasmic crescendo of sexual fulfillment intertwined with her love of God. She knows that nothing's going to happen to her if she does what she believes is right. She wakes up, goes to jail, tells the police the man is innocent, and he is freed. Then everybody takes a bow as if to say we all play a part in this little scenario."

Yet the real impact of the video is concentrated in the sometimes startling visual images already mentioned.

In the press, rumblings and repercussions from religious figures started almost immediately after the release of the video.

The Reverend Donald Wildmon, executive director of American Family Association, a 380,000 congregation, wrote that the video featured "disrespect and disdain for the religious beliefs of millions of Americans." It was "steeped in Christian symbolism in general and Roman Catholic symbolism specifically," he went on. "The video's symbolism of sexuality, suggesting that priests (and indeed all Christians) are sexually repressed, is blatantly offensive."

In Wildmon's view Madonna represented Christ in the video and "is shown in a scene suggesting that she has sex with the priest, obviously to free him from sexual repression. That is absolutely repugnant to Christians."

He also quoted a statement made by Madonna and published in *Penthouse:* "Crucifixes are sexy because there's a naked man on them." "For the next year," Wildmon concluded, "I will not drink Pepsi. If enough others join me, perhaps respect for religious beliefs of others will be helped tremendously. At least it is a start."

At first Pepsi-Cola put up a brave front, confining its company remarks to the commercial in which none of the above profanities occurred. Pepsi pointed out that it was "delighted" with the television commercial. Even after there were protests in Europe over Madonna's "Like a Prayer" video, the company stood by her.

"We'll probably reintroduce the commercials when the song hits the top of the charts," said Pepsi's Todd MacKenzie. "I won't lay out our media buy, but that's what we did for Michael Jackson."

He said Pepsi was "absolutely thrilled with the commercials," which were shown on all three networks and reached some 250 million people worldwide. The brave front persisted for about a month. However, when Wildmon called for a boycott of Pepsi from his 380,000 parishoners, Pepsi began getting calls from distributors. Other protesters soon joined the queue behind Wildmon's group.

Finally when the Pepsi brass saw what had been unleashed by their use of Madonna in her commercial for them, they decided to cancel it. The final decision was announced on April 4, about a month after the commercial first rolled.

Pepsi's rationale for pulling the ad, which, as it correctly pointed out, was entirely blameless, was that consumers—that is, people who might be or might not be buying Pepsi-Cola—might "confuse" the message of the video with the message of the commercial. The point was: "Why fuel that confusion? It was better to call it a day."

Pepsi saw it as a bad interaction of events. In a side note the company admitted that it had not demanded to see the video before it was aired. "The artist was not obliged to show the video to us," an unidentified spokesperson said. "Of course, if we go this route again, we'll want to probe for these kinds of things."

Indeed, yes.

It was a lesson that cost Pepsico Inc. a purported five million dollars—which Madonna kept!

Ironically enough, shortly after Pepsi canceled the commercial, another fundamentalist group—a rival to Wildmon's bunch—called for Pepsi to start showing the ad again!

"Pepsi is the choice of the fundamentalist generation," said Jim Luce, executive director and cofounder of Fundamentalists Anonymous, a New York–based organization of former Christian fundamentalists. "Pepsi didn't make a marketing decision. It simply succumbed to the intimidation of a fundamentalist group."

Luce, with his tongue firmly in his cheek, said his group would begin a national campaign to get Pepsi to air the ad again. The campaign would introduce a lineup of "big-time losers" to endorse Pepsi. "By the time we're through," said Richard Yao, cofounder of Fundamentalists Anonymous, "only losers will drink Pepsi."

Did "Fundamentalists Anonymous" actually exist? one began to wonder. Or was its "campaign" simply a jesting commentary on the absurdity of the public-relations flap unleashed by Madonna's music video?

The album *Like a Prayer* itself went down well with the music critics. *The Washington Post*'s Richard Harrington wrote,

" 'Like a Prayer' is a solid album that will not disappoint [Madonna's] fans and may actually challenge them and her detractors. Madonna has made a habit of reinventing herself on a regular basis: This time around she's decided to open her heart, and in so doing, she's also opened her art. Some critics may sniff at the effort; consumers may actually sniff the record and find that love stinks like patchouli. 'Like a Prayer' offers Madonna's takes on letting go—of Sean, of family, of religion—and coming to terms with the consequences of her release. It reflects a certain courage, and while that doesn't always lead to good songs, it's a thoroughly commendable effort.

"So there we have it, the new, improved Madonna."

In the end the album *Like a Prayer*, showing Madonna on the cover dressed like a cross between a hippie and a gypsy, sold eleven million copies—equaling the success of her best-selling *Like a Virgin*.

18

COMIC-STRIP ROMANCE

On Madonna's very first date with Sean Penn he took her to a party being given by the actor Warren Beatty, Shirley MacLaine's kid brother.

"It was an auspicious evening," Madonna told a *Vanity Fair* writer. "I met my friends Sandra Bernhard and Warren Beatty on the same evening on my first date with Sean. He was introducing me to all his friends. Basically, *he* was friends with Warren, not me."

That brief meeting with Warren Beatty served Madonna in good stead several years later, in 1989, when Beatty was putting together the movie based on Chester Gould's comic strip, *Dick Tracy*. Those plans were shrouded in secrecy for at least a year at Walt Disney Pictures in Hollywood.

In all, it took *Dick Tracy* almost fifteen years to come to the screen after the idea of making a picture was first conceived. In 1975 the rights were owned by producer Michael Laughlin, who finally gave up his option on the strip when no one would commit to it. Floyd Mutrux and Art Linson optioned the property two years later.

Then Paramount, where producers Michael Eisner and Jeffrey Katzenberg were working, became interested. In 1983

Universal Pictures and Paramount mutually backed out of a joint agreement to produce the film.

In all, four top-notch directors tried to get the project off the ground, including Martin Scorsese, Jon Landis, and Richard Benjamin. At one point Clint Eastwood wanted to play Tracy, although by then Beatty had first refusal on the role.

In fact Beatty almost made the movie with Walter Hill directing, but Hill characteristically wanted total realism, while Beatty wanted a comic-strip fantasy that would re-create his own childhood impression of the strip.

Beatty became impatient and bought the rights himself in 1985 and settled on a script that had already been written by Jim Cash and Jack Epps, Jr.—a script that had been commissioned earlier by Linson and Mutrux when they held the property.

The script was not to be the finished shooting script at all. Beatty and Bo Goldman rewrote significant parts of the dialogue, but lost a Writers Guild arbitration and never received screen credit. Their names, however, appeared on the paperback "novelization" of the script.

By the time Beatty acquired the rights, he was in a negative position as far as it came to gaining studio attention for the main role. He had suffered an absolute disaster in his production of the film *Ishtar,* which bombed but good in 1987. Prior to that he had peaked in the production of *Reds* in 1981, in which he starred and which he directed.

He had to find his way back into the successful big time. And he thought he had found it in the Dick Tracy concept. So, he began peddling the idea himself. By that time Katzenberg and Eisner had moved to Walt Disney Pictures and were still interested in doing *Tracy.* Katzenberg had become chairman of the board at Disney.

Hearing about Beatty's interest, Katzenberg said, "We went after Beatty." He remembered, "Warren has wanted to make this movie for ten years."

But getting together with Beatty was no breeze. The actor was not an easy man to deal with. Nor was the studio an easy organization to deal with. Beatty, on his part, was a perfectionist who had never been known to skimp on spending money to achieve quality. And Disney, on its part, was a studio that had become famous for making big films with big stars on the cheap.

The agreement was eighteen months in the making. In the end the cost and the concept were finally agreed to, including provisions for a sequel. In the deal was a clause that Beatty would bring in the picture for twenty-five million dollars.

Beatty's initial concept for the film was to put on the big screen, with all the film industry's advances and its highest production values, a realistic make-believe combination of a crime-city action picture and the epic legend of a little boy's dream hero.

Chester Gould had everything in the comic strip—even a true love for Dick Tracy, named, by no accident, Tess Trueheart. There was also a seductive nightclub entertainer named Breathless Mahoney.

In a crime-fighting film today it is necessary for at least a modicum of blood to be shed. But it was Beatty's intention from the beginning not to show a drop of blood. In addition, he had an obsession about colors and decided that since this was a filmic vision of a comic strip, all colors should be primary ones—with sets and costumes designed in basic tints.

Casting was fun. Al Pacino became the kingpin of crime, "Big Boy" Caprice. Dustin Hoffman was cast as Mumbles, one of Gould's more famous characters. James Caan—Sonny in the original *Godfather* (in which Pacino also starred)—was Ribs, another Gould character.

It is not really clear exactly how Madonna came to be cast in the role of Breathless Mahoney. According to her, she simply put on the pressure, and the rest, as they say, is history.

"I called up Warren," she said, "and told him I really wanted [the part of Breathless]. I saw the A list, and I was on the Z list. I felt like a jerk."

Exactly how she managed to convince Beatty that she should be Breathless instead of a hundred other actresses is not clear. But she did it. Not only did she become Chester Gould's Breathless Mahoney, but she also became Warren Beatty's Madonna (Ciccone). Two roles for the price of one.

Even before Madonna was cast in the role, it was obvious that the concept of Breathless Mahoney had to be changed. In Gould's comic strip she was a dangerous and atrocious little bitch. When she first appeared in the strip sometime in 1946, she was a psychopathic thief who had stabbed a man in the back with a huge pair of pruning shears. Eventually, after all her posturing and titillating of the great detective, she managed to dump rat poison into a cup of coffee, which she served lovingly to him.

So, the scriptwriters worked at the character making her more or less a simple siren and vamp, even though she still retained her own evil interior psychic values. Indeed, as is fitting in any kind of fairy tale, Breathless/Madonna temporarily became a maiden in distress straight out of fantasy literature, in spite of her panting desire for the knight in shining armor. It was only after she had served her purpose in intriguing Tracy that her true motives were allowed to come out.

"I could see a lot of myself in Breathless," Madonna said, "and a lot of Breathless in me. After reading all the material available, talking to the people involved, absorbing the drama, I knew it was a part I was meant to play. I felt that it wasn't enough just to act out a two-dimensional comic-[strip] part—I had to bring Breathless to life, let her live for a little while in the real world, you know?"

In all, "Breathless is a character who obviously spends more time in bed than anywhere else, and has to be portrayed that way."

To fulfill the plot requirements, "Breathless thinks there's a weakness in Tracy somewhere, and if she can reach it, she has her freedom. She, I, make an all-out effort. It's a fun, uninhibited part to play. Posing where you know light streams through your clothes, striking those positions that advertise everything you've got—what girl wouldn't like to have the part?"

But, of course, "I wanted the role, too, because of Warren Beatty. He *is* Dick Tracy, isolated, intelligent, observant, all the traits a detective needs, and with talents to guarantee a good picture, and a good boost to a working career. I gave it my best shot."

It wasn't easy. Beatty put her to the test right away. He told her that she had to change her hair color. He wanted her to be a blonde, as Breathless was in the strip. Madonna had recently turned herself back into a brunette. She pleaded with him not to make her go back to that earlier shade.

"I felt kind of great having my own hair color for the first time in years. And then I had to change it, so I had a bit of an identity crisis. Being blond is definitely a state of mind. I feel more grounded, and Italian, when I have dark hair. Being blond has some incredible sort of sexual connotation. Men really respond to it."

Beatty was adamant. She surrendered. She wanted this role to be her best to date. She knew she had a chance this time. She hoped that she had finally found the perfect film to make it back to the plateau she had reached with the release of her first major film, *Desperately Seeking Susan.*

"I've learned that if you surround yourself with great writers and great actors and a great director . . . it's pretty hard to go wrong. In the past I've been in a really big hurry to make movies and I haven't taken the time to make sure all of those elements were in line. It's a waste of time doing something mediocre."

As for the costuming of Breathless/Madonna, the picture's designer, Milena Canonero, wanted her to represent the night, the moon, and—you guessed it—sex. She designed Madonna's clothes in black, midnight blue, or in silver to suggest a moonbeam. Of course the costumes were tight and revealing, one dress cut so low that Madonna kept falling out of it during rehearsals.

This led Beatty to a typical tongue-in-cheek jape: "She's dressed in a way that accentuates her good health."

As for her style of singing, Madonna incorporated a brand-new—for her—line of delivery, what might simply be called a "stroll down Melody Lane," to keep the musical background of the story in line with Beatty's concept of the comic-strip past. In other words, she dropped the rock-and-roll and funky present and sang in the style of the thirties and forties.

In her tight contract with Beatty Madonna had reserved the right to write and sing songs on her own that were inspired by her part in the movie. The songs in the movie were written by Stephen Sondheim.

One of his fast numbers was a two-beat background to a tap dance. The words had to do with being so happy with life as it was that the singer simply wanted more of the same.

In "Sooner or Later," the singer stated that once she had kissed a man, he never tried to fight her again. But she was a good girl at heart—beneath the false image of the vamp—one who would love a man, and love him alone.

In "What Can You Lose?" Sondheim created a duet that Madonna sang with Mandy Patinkin, cast in the picture as her piano accompanist.

To sing these songs of Sondheim's, Madonna had to widen her vocal range to a degree and came through as a thoroughly competent singer, quite an advance over her earlier work. However, it was obvious that the show tunes she was singing called for just a bit more range and agility than she actually had.

She admitted that in the long run the most difficult part about playing the role of Breathless Mahoney was to learn to sing the Stephen Sondheim songs.

"He writes songs to the beat of a different drummer," she explained. "Most songs, you can make a good guess [as to] what's coming next, three guesses will always give you the right answer. Stephen writes like nobody else, and where his song is going is *anybody's* guess. Even after you know them, they sound unfamiliar, and that makes them hard to learn and sing."

One thing Madonna did not have to worry about was wearing the prosthetic rubber masks that most of the exaggerated comic-strip characters in the picture were forced to live in. Nor did Glenne Headly, who played Tess Trueheart. Nor did Tracy, of course, in his yellow raincoat and trademark fedora.

The foam-rubber masks took about an hour and a half to three and a half hours to apply—each day! Then, the actors would have to wear them for twelve hours of filming.

"My eyes itched and hurt," complained R. G. Armstrong, who played Pruneface, another famous Gould character. "I'd keep them closed until I'd shoot, just to give them a rest."

Al Pacino had to see a dermatologist for shots and anti-biotics because of the mask he wore. So did Ed O'Ross, who played Gould's character Itchy. The company had to shoot around these two actors for three weeks.

Dick Van Dyke, who played a district attorney without a mask, broke his shoulder when he fell after being shot in a scene. "Fortunately, by the time I broke it, we'd already done five or six takes, so they had what they needed."

Most of the props were in comic-strip style, too, in order, as Beatty explained, to give the film that thirties comic-page feeling. For example a bottle of whiskey was simply labeled WHISKEY in big caps. A dollar bill had a dollar sign right in the middle of it. The wooden furniture was treated so that it would show no grain, exactly the way furniture looks in the comics.

"Specifics would kill the soul of the piece," said production designer Richard Sylbert, who tried to carry out Beatty's demands for comic-strip reality.

Madonna had been absolutely serious on her contract with Beatty—particularly about reserving the right to write and sing songs of her own that were inspired by her part in the movie.

In all, she and Patrick Leonard turned out five songs "inspired" by the picture. They were not released until the film came out, although they were prepared beforehand and at the ready for the picture's opening date.

The subjects were intrinsically Madonnaesque: There were songs of desire, both carnal and material. There were songs of power ploys. There were songs of the shifty nature of people, good to bad, especially as applied to women.

For example, "He's a Man," written by Madonna and Leonard, was typically vampish. The lyrics said that Madonna knew all about what having fun was—and she knew how to have it. That sentiment was definitely a lightweight one compared to other numbers she and Leonard produced.

The lyrics of "Hanky Panky," backed up by a big-band blues treatment, concerned sexual spanking. The singer entreated her lover to handle her like a "bad girl," even though she was being good to him. She did not want his thanks; what she wanted was to be lightly spanked.

In "Back to Business," Madonna used a line from the film's

scenario in the lyrics—about not knowing if her man wanted to hit her or to kiss her. Once she even echoed the spanking theme of "Hanky Panky" by saying that her bottom hurt simply by *thinking* about being spanked.

The Madonna/Leonard tunes generally adhered to the pop format of the thirties and forties, unlike the Sondheim songs, which were strictly—well—Sondheimish.

The motion picture *Dick Tracy* was shot under great secrecy on closely guarded sets in Burbank, California, at the Disney studios. The very first thing that happened when it was discovered that Madonna was in the cast of the picture was that the press immediately leapt to the conclusion that she and Warren Beatty had become an "item."

They had indeed.

How *much* of an item, of course, was in the minds of the beholders.

In a profile on Warren Beatty in *Rolling Stone,* Bill Zehme wrote, "We only see Warren when he loves deeply (we only *hear* about him when he prowls)." It was in 1989, Zehme wrote, that Beatty told someone confidentially at a luncheon, "Sometimes I look at myself in the mirror and say, *'I'm with Madonna!' "*

"It is a comic-strip romance," Zehme wrote about the purported Madonna/Beatty affair. "They are cozy together in a prickly sort of way. Their pet names for each other are 'Old Man' and 'Buzzbomb.' "

All kidding aside, there *was* an affair, of course, as there would normally be between two such available people as Madonna and Warren Beatty. But this was a professional liaison as well as a personal one, and the professional level was never totally vacated. Beatty, for his part, was extremely impressed with Madonna's professionalism in attacking the role of Breathless Mahoney.

"I think Madonna has energy, beauty, humor, talent, intelligence," he told *Vanity Fair.* "And I think the most surprising thing about her after I had worked with her was to see the level of diligence that she has. She really works hard."

Madonna also learned a great deal from working with Beatty.

"I think you want the approval of anybody you're having

a relationship with, and even if I wasn't with Warren I would want his approval because he's a brilliant guy. I think seventy-five percent of the country wants Warren Beatty's approval."

She added, "He's been with the world's most beautiful, most glamorous, talented women. I go, 'Oh, my God! Oh, my God!' That's one part of me. I mean, how can I ever be as fabulous as Brigitte Bardot when she was twenty-five? Or Natalie Wood? Or any of those people? Then there is the other side of me that says I'm better than all of them."

In spite of that statement Beatty sometimes thought he had more respect for Madonna than she had for herself. "I don't know that there are many people who can do as many things as Madonna can do as well. People who are in a positive frame of mind, who bring as much energy and willingness to work as Madonna does. She has, in this respect, a real healthy humility about the theater. I think this is a prime requisite to be able to function in theater—or, actually, in art."

About her artistic forays into sexuality, Beatty said, "Well, I think she's courageous in the areas that she explores artistically. I think that's what she wants to explore. . . . Off the top of my head, [Madonna's] generous spirit would be the thing I think that informs her work the most. As she goes on, she will gain the artistic respect that she already deserves."

Madonna had no idea how long their relationship would last. "I have moments when I'm really romantic and I think, 'We're just perfect together.' He's just past so much bullshit. He has an outlook on life, an overview, that I don't have, and I think that makes for something that will last." She went on, "He's very protective. He's not easily shocked, either—which is great—by the things that have happened to me."

The romance between the two of them spluttered out once the movie was released. There were rumors that Beatty was unfaithful to her—which was certainly in character. When Madonna felt used, she had her own way of getting back at him.

MADONNA: Warren, did you *really* chase that girl for a year?
BEATTY: Nah! It's all lies.

Was it? "I should have known better," Madonna admitted. "I was unrealistic, but then, you always think you're going to be the one."

The relationship broke off with a reprise of the old Hollywood punchline:

BEATTY: You're fired!
MADONNA: You can't fire me, I quit!

"It's a really hard thing to accept in life that no matter what you do you can't change a person. If you say, 'I don't want you looking at that woman,' they're going to do it anyway," Madonna reasoned. "You want to think that if this person is in love with you, you have control over them. But you don't. And to accept that in life is next to impossible."

MADONNA: I want to be a fly on the wall for all of Warren Beatty's conversations, but I wouldn't want the reverse.

According to Lynn Hirschberg in *Vanity Fair*, there was a consensus of opinion among some friends of both Beatty and Madonna that he was simply using her to promote his movie.

Dick Tracy opened on June 15, 1990, to several good days of box office, but then seemed to lose steam. The reviews were uniformly good—it was the audience that didn't seem to be there in the seats. It still brought in a cool hundred million dollars during the season, however.

Newsweek's David Ansen critiqued the movie for a sidebar story, grading it about a B+. He noted that the film itself, which could have been a turkey, was "pretty darn swell." He laid its excellence to the creative daring of Warren Beatty, asking, "Who else would stage an action montage to the slow rhythms of a Stephen Sondheim song?"

Madonna, he wrote, was "smashingly unsubtle as the femme fatale—quivering with lust, double-entendres, and bad intentions." He said that she bridged the past to Monroe, Dietrich, and others, and sang quite a bit like her contemporary Bernadette Peters.

"This is no ready-to-wear movie; it's the work of a cinematic couturier. Take it for what it is: a simple gift, consummately wrapped."

In a companion piece on feminists in movies, *The New York Times*'s Janet Maslin noted of Madonna, "No one will ever accuse Madonna of being compliant, but her Breathless Mahoney in *Dick Tracy* is the very model of superavailable femme fatale. Madonna, who strikes this exaggeratedly seductive pose without any discernible passion of her own, once again walks a disturbingly fine line between parodying and pandering," with a kind of "deadpan simpering."

An interesting fact was publicized when the movie opened. Madonna had worked for scale—$1,440 a week—on *Dick Tracy*. Beatty got $9 million up-front, against 10 percent of the profits (not the gross).

But that was the *surface* reporting. Actually Madonna had negotiated a percentage of the box-office revenues from the film, video, and merchandise sales that was worth about five million dollars. *And*, as has been mentioned, she arranged to release a number of songs "inspired" by the movie on her own album, which was to make her about fourteen million.

In the long run it was actually Beatty who stood short.

"I'm not going to overlook the fact that [being in *Dick Tracy* is] a great opportunity for me, too," Madonna said. "Most people don't associate me with movies. But I know I have a much bigger following than Warren does and a lot of my audience isn't even aware of who he is."

Touché.

The video for Madonna's "Like a Prayer" was so controversial that Pepsi was forced to cancel a campaign that was to feature the singer and the song.

Madonna, seen with her post-Warren boyfriend, the artist model Tony Ward (*right*)

Madonna and her friend Sandra Bernhard raised questions a to how close they really were after they performed a hip grinding duet at this charity benefit.

Her relationship with Warren Beatty turned out to be one of the most closely watched Hollywood pairings in recent memory.

Madonna stunned audiences who attended her *Blonde Ambition* tour when she came out in Jean-Paul Gaultier creations like this one.

Madonna "climaxed" each performance of "Like a Virgin" by simulating masturbation on a scarlet double bed.

When Madonna performed for her hometown crowd, she sang "Happy Birthday" to her dad, Silvio Ciccone, in front of twenty thousand screaming fans.

Madonna attends the Film Critics Awards with the director of her film *Truth or Dare*, Alex Keshishian.

Madonna with on-again off-again boyfriend Tony Ward in the "Justify My Love" video. Its gender-bending scenes were so steamy that MTV refused to show it.

Madonna performs "Sooner or Later (I Always Get My Man)" from the film *Dick Tracy* during the 63rd Annual Academy Awards show. The song won the Oscar, and Madonna's Marilyn tribute brought down the house.

19

Ambitious Blonde

Although she had never returned to her habit of spending most of her nights in discotheques and dance halls as she had in her first years in Manhattan, Madonna did drop in occasionally to observe and participate in the more esoteric black and Latino dance clubs. It was there that she became intrigued by a "new" dance craze called Vogue. Dancing a Vogue number meant suddenly striking a frozen pose in the middle of a step, holding it for some ten to fifteen seconds, and then continuing the dance movements.

The concept struck Madonna as something to hold in mind for a future video or dance routine. At the time she was just putting the finishing touches to the *Dick Tracy* album, containing the three Sondheim tunes from the film plus some numbers she had written to tie in with the picture. The album itself would be titled *I'm Breathless: Music from and Inspired by the Film "Dick Tracy."*

What she needed was a specialty number to kick off the

album itself—something that incorporated the elements of *Dick Tracy* without stemming directly or indirectly from it.

Nostalgia was the keystone of the film. Warren Beatty had seen to that. Now Madonna decided to make obeisance to nostalgia too, a concept of nostalgia that would take quite a different turn from his.

Calling the number "Vogue," she cowrote it with dance remixer Shep Pettibone, and incorporated the freeze-frame aspect of the Vogue dance step with various other elements of Beatty's nostalgic overview.

In doing so, she created another brand-new Madonna. Her new public image was shaped on at least three levels of perception: sound, sight, and subliminal association. The "sound" involved the background music and Madonna's voice. The "sight" involved the startling images—the frozen poses—she used to make the video different. The "subliminal association" involved her constant reminder of famous film entertainers of the past.

But it was the gimmick of the Vogue dance step that *made* the video of the number—and finally made the album itself stand out.

The "Vogue" video was shot in stark black and white, an obvious bow to the golden age of film. The camera first pans through the large room of what appears to be a haunted mansion, in which a dozen wealthy, well-dressed aristocrat types are standing frozen like waxwork figures in statuelike poses. The camera suddenly intercuts a view of Madonna's back.

She turns around face on to the camera and starts singing a lyric about life being rough, but it can't be all black because there's one place where everything is marvelous—on the dance floor! So, get out there and start moving to the rhythm of the music.

Then suddenly Madonna freezes in a dramatic tableau. "Strike a pose!" she commands. She is introducing the Vogue. In her pose Madonna becomes statuesque, glamorous, blond, and unattainable. She is a true reprise of the thirties and forties screen queen, adapting herself to the role of a siren out of the past. The virginal ice maiden—all blond, aloof, and remote—is a brand-new "pose" for Madonna.

And she makes it stick.

Interspersed among the Madonna poses in "Vogue" are subliminal references to the great movie faces of the past. In fact each pose itself generally brings to mind one of the more famous of those "great faces." Madonna is Marilyn Monroe, almost as much as she was Monroe in her earlier "Material Girl" video.

She switches to rap, talking about the style and grace of the early Hollywood stars.

Next come names, names, names, as the rap continues, mentioning Greta Garbo, Marilyn Monroe, Marlene Dietrich, Joe DiMaggio, Marlon Brando, and Jimmy Dean.

Plus: Katharine Hepburn, Bette Davis, Jean Harlow, Rita Hayworth, Fred Astaire, Gene Kelly, and Ginger Rogers as men and women with allure and glamour.

She had, in the words of Anne Ayers, *USA Today*'s music editor in a *TV Guide* piece, "become pop music's reigning female power." And Ayers also wrote, "It's in video that Madonna's mysterious quicksilver essence seems to have found its best expression."

"When you make a video," said Abbey Konowitch, MTV's senior vice president for music and talent, "you try to capture the mood of a song. But Madonna takes it to the next level to challenge the viewer with her art, her look, her dancing."

About Madonna, he said, "There are few artists who own the art form. She's at the top."

The "posing" in "Vogue" was annoying to some. *USA Today*'s Edna Gunderson called the step a "trendy Manhattan-born dance of peacockish poses." But, she admitted, "It's trickier than it looks; without confidence and control, the practitioner resembles a clumsy traffic cop."

Mike LaSalle, of the *San Francisco Chronicle*, found the "posing" gimmick tiresome: " 'Strike a pose, there's nothing to it,' Madonna sings. This is an original concept. It eliminates movement and interaction and reduces dance to its purest element: narcissistic exhibitionism. . . . Madonna's good at it." He noted, "The start and stop quality of 'Vogue' makes it a little like Aerobic Internal training."

The more sophisticated music critics reviewed the album,

giving top ratings to the Stephen Sondheim numbers: "Sooner or Later," "What Can You Lose?" and "More." And they liked "Vogue," even as an audio. But Jon Pareles of *The New York Times* wrote, "Anyone who buys *I'm Breathless* expecting more of the same [as in 'Vogue'] will feel like the victim of a bait-and-switch maneuver."

As predicted, the album started selling briskly as soon as it appeared.

On May Day 1990 Madonna appeared on Arsenio Hall's popular talk show. She had created a minor sensation the year before when she had danced at a benefit for the Brooklyn Academy of Music Opera House in a program titled "Don't Bungle the Jungle"—the money was going to help save the planet from extinction by pollution—along with an old friend of hers, Sandra Bernhard.

In the grand-finale duet of "I Got You, Babe"—hauntingly familiar as the song Sonny and Cher used to sing together years before on television—the two women had gone through a long series of crotchgrabbing, bumps, grinds, and other Madonna-like actions, and got a rousing ovation from the crowd of two thousand.

Then, almost deliberately, since Madonna had hinted on the David Letterman television talk show that she might have lesbian ambitions toward Sandra Bernhard, the two dancers wrapped their arms around each other and hugged, making the crowd gasp in shock.

"Don't believe these stories!" Madonna shouted with a laugh.

Bernhard leered at the crowd. "*Believe* those stories!"

So, when she appeared on the Hall show, the audience—and Hall—were primed for *anything*.

"My mother is a big fan of yours," the host began in a velvet-glove approach. "She saw your video and she called me and said, 'What does she mean, "Gives good face?" ' "

Madonna hardly blinked. "Well," she responded, "it's not exactly like giving——" And the last words were bleeped out—hardly a mystery what she said.

"You really know how to create controversy," Hall said. "I saw a picture of you the other day, and one breast was hanging out."

"If you've got it," Madonna retorted, "flaunt it. Right?"

Later Hall got into the song "Hanky Panky," which was creating some stir in its advocacy of sexual spanking. "What *is* the song about?"

"I'm talking about the spanking you get when you're good."

"Yeah. Okay. Dr. Ruth and I touched on this subject one night."

"Where did you touch?" Madonna shot back quickly.

"Well, actually," Hall said, playing along with the gag, "I bent her over like this and touched right about—right about there."

"I bet you *she* could tell you about getting a spanking."

"Oh, yes. Yes. I like to spank her and call her 'Baby Ruth.' "

Then Hall asked, "What kind of things make you jealous? Like does the name Joan Collins make you jealous?"

"No," Madonna snapped. "Have you seen her lately?"

The name Sandra Bernhard was bound to come up, and it did. "There's a rumor about you and Sandra Bernhard. What do you like about Sandra?"

"She's funny," Madonna said.

Toward the end of the broadcast it was Madonna's turn. "You know, if anybody—any of my dancers—got their hair cut like yours, they couldn't be in my show."

Hall was cool but annoyed. "Why is that?"

"Because it's tired."

Hall responded, "Now, what should I have? Hair like Warren [Beatty]?"

On the show Hall kept his mouth shut, but later he stated in an interview that he was really thinking, "Let's not let this Caucasian bleached blonde be the judge of black hair fashion!"

As she left the set, Madonna got in another lick at her host and his taste in furniture. "These couches have to go! When you drive down the street . . . and these couches are in the window, it always says, 'Half Off.' "

"She's dogging me at every turn!" moaned Hall.

Madonna's presence made it Arsenio Hall's highest-rated show to that date.

Somehow, she seemed to be all over the tube in 1990. In an attempt in late 1989 to rev up her motion picture career, she had played in a four-part anthology film composed of Damon Runyon stories. She was cast opposite Randy Quaid in a segment from *Bloodhounds of Broadway,* produced for art-house screening by American Playhouse and eventually shown on PBS in 1990.

Runyon was the Broadway columnist who in the twenties turned his hand to short fiction and created a unique style of big-city narration. He invented his own New York slang: "croak" (to die), "dukes" (fists), "equalizer" (gun), "hot spot" (predicament), "blower" (phone), and even "drop dead" a few years before Judy Holliday uttered it on Broadway.

The Madonna role in the foursome was that of Hortense Hathaway, one of the "dolls" playing opposite Randy Quaid's Feet Samuels. The plot of the segment, titled "A Very Honorable Guy," revolves around a rather odd dilemma. Samuels has sold his exceptionally large feet to science—actually to a doctor. The doctor, apparently a reincarnation of Shylock, expects delivery the very next day—and won't take them except *as they are,* attached to the rest of his body.

The reviews of the film, which eventually aired in May 1990 on Public Television, were hardly uniform.

Paul Henniger, *San Francisco Chronicle:* "Another great journalist once said, 'There are eight million stories in the Naked City.' American Playhouse has packaged just four of them in splendid fashion."

Vincent Canby, *The New York Times:* "*Bloodhounds of Broadway* never gets going."

Ray Loynd, *Los Angeles Times:* "Madonna, playing a showgirl flapper and coiffed like a Louise Brooks Kewpie-doll, briefly enlivens the Damon Runyon–inspired *Bloodhounds of Broadway.*"

Clifford Terry, *Chicago Tribune:* "A quirkily stylized, brittle film that was recut after the death of director Howard Brookner, it has some nice moments, but never really makes it. Madonna, though, gives a quiet, understated performance."

In October 1989 Madonna had approached the Nike Company to discuss a product-endorsement deal, much like the one that had turned so sour in Pepsi-Cola's hands. She was hoping to endorse a new dance shoe. Nike offered her four and a quarter million dollars to do it.

The negotiations continued through a period of six months, but in March everything fell apart because of what was loosely called "scheduling problems"—free translation: Nobody really knew what went wrong.

From insiders the real story eventually emerged. Madonna was becoming increasingly reluctant to have herself photographed as actually endorsing, personally, the "property." That is, apparently she did not want to wear the shoes while she was dancing. One Nike executive put it bluntly, "She wouldn't put them on her feet."

When the negotiators backed out, Madonna felt that she had made a mistake in tactics somewhere along the line. The story got out that she began putting in personal telephone calls to Philip Knight, the chairman of Nike's board. She wanted to revive the deal.

Knight did not fall for that. And when he turned a deaf ear to Madonna's pleas, her lawyers stepped in, voicing a threat to sue Nike for the four and a quarter million involved, even though no commercial had yet been produced or worked on.

In July 1990 Madonna was preparing for the biggest world tour she had ever projected. In order to underwrite some of the costs, she contacted Nike's bête noire, their biggest competitor, Reebok International, the makers of shoes similar to Nike's.

Reebok had produced a television commercial through its ad agency, Chiat/Day/Mojo, involving two spots showing stunt men wearing sneakers "bungee jumping" from a bridge with tethers tied to one ankle. Even on film the action comes across as frightening, the jumpers engaged in a long free-fall from a high place and then jerked upside down by the tightening of the thongs on their ankles. Revised versions were made, but the jump was too scary to be acceptable to ordinary viewers. Two of the three major networks refused to show the spots. In the end Reebok and Chiat/Day/Mojo ate the costs and canceled the spots.

Part of Chiat/Day/Mojo's Reebok account was taken over

by Hill, Holliday, Connors, Cosmopulos, Boston. And it was that agency that dealt with Madonna. It was hoped by Reebok that Madonna would endorse the performance and life-style products of the firm.

Steven Levitt, president of Marketing Evaluations TVQ Inc., a firm that rated the popularity of celebrities, told Reebok that Madonna was "widely known—but not particularly liked—by the public." Levitt said, "As a celebrity, an overwhelming majority of people are turned off to her." But of course, he admitted, she remained popular with teenagers.

By May 1990 it looked as if the Reebok deal might go through. A confirmation in *Advertising Age* of a Reebok agreement voiced by Kenneth R. Lightcap was almost immediately nulled. "I jumped the gun," Lightcap admitted. "We haven't signed a thing yet."

Things were marching steadily toward a solid and happy conclusion of a deal that month, reportedly paying close to six million dollars to Madonna for a commercial for Reebok. Both sides had agreed to the terms and to the involved details of the agreement. The only thing that remained was for the papers to be signed.

And then—

On May 29, 1990, Warner Bros. released Madonna's single from the *I'm Breathless* album titled "Hanky Panky." Almost immediately there were loud squawks phoned in to the radio stations that played it.

"We've been getting a lot of complaint calls," the music director of Boston's WXKS-FM said. "We got a lot of calls from women who were concerned about the lyrical content."

Madonna's words had it that everyone liked different things, and as for her, she liked to be spanked lightly and lovingly.

She then mentioned that instead of being sweet-talked or teased, she liked her hands tied behind her back; that, to her, was the height of pleasure.

It was, in short, a song that celebrated sexual spanking.

And that focused media attention on Reebok and its pending deal. "For any company considering using Madonna, decisions should be made on . . . how you manage the deal,"

Bernadette Mansur, Reebok's spokesperson, said. "Madonna is a megastar. She is currently selling out concerts all around the world. She is associated with fitness and fashion and is on the cutting edge, and thus would be a choice for any consumer marketing company interested in promoting their product."

A former vice president for marketing at Reebok spoke up. "If I were there, I wouldn't want her," said Stephen J. Encarnacao. "There's no question she is a superstar." But "I would think that the potential of risk is perhaps greater than the potential of reward at this point, given the controversial direction she is going in. Any kind of talent that turns off as large a segment of parents and as large a segment of kids as she does is risky."

Jack Connors, president of Hill, Holliday et al., Reebok's advertising agency, disagreed. Getting noticed, he pointed out, was what advertising on the crowded airwaves is all about. "Leadership requires that once in a while you go out to the edge," he said. "In this particular case we have to be sure that we don't go *over* the edge."

He said, "Madonna is a very hot property for a lot of reasons. Some of them are very positive, and those will be the reasons we go with if we work with Madonna. There's too much equity at Reebok for them to jeopardize their reputation over one actor or actress who may or may not have done a song that people call into question."

A brave front.

Two months later Reebok pulled out of its arrangement with Madonna. "Madonna's availability and our need to get her weren't a mesh," Mansur said in the convoluted prose of promotion puffery. "We needed to get some benefits out of it to continue with the deal."

Another consultant at Celebrity Endorsement Network supported Reebok's negative decision. "Between [Madonna's] films, her concerts, and her love affairs, I'm sure there would be a problem with most advertisers. It takes a very special advertiser to take these kinds of risks."

The year 1990 was the year of Madonna's biggest world tour yet, the one she called "Blonde Ambition." "Ambition" was in fact a transference of Madonna's own ambition, and thus honestly titled. It was an anthology of all her best stage work and, in her own words, was "much more theatrical than anything I've ever done."

The concert featured eighteen songs and spanned her entire career, introducing new songs from the *I'm Breathless* album as well. Madonna, the icon, was becoming more a Ciccone icon; she hired her brother, Christopher Ciccone, to act as art director for the show's sets.

To come up with the designs, the two of them—sister and brother—took a crash course in the fashion and architecture of the twenties, thirties, and forties. Then, after deciding on a rough order for the show, Ciccone drew sketches and sent them to Madonna.

"We disagreed on a lot of things, but she trusts me," he said. He designed the sets for Madonna, he said, since the show *was* Madonna. "The audience looks at what she might be sitting on, or rubbing up against, or where her hand might be. The set *enhances* her."

The tour itself started in Japan, then returned to the United States, where thirty-two stops were made, including Canada, and then moved on to Europe, where a bit of controversial action took place.

Although Italy had been receptive to her "Who's That Girl?" tour in 1988, prominent Catholics began branding the "Blond Ambition" concert as "offensive," apparently from reports from Catholics in the United States. An attempt was made to shut down the tour and keep it from reaching Rome. A Catholic news agency, which reflected opinions of the Italian Bishops' Conference, criticized her use of crucifixes and sacred symbols in concerts and videos.

Famiglia Domani (The Family Tomorrow), a Catholic lobby group, said that it had written to Ugo Poletti, the cardinal of Rome, requesting him to "stop this shameful spectacle [from] taking place in Rome—a city dear to millions of Catholics."

Then just before Madonna arrived, the July 11 concert was suddenly called off—because of a threatened general strike. The strike was then called off, and the concert was rescheduled.

When Madonna landed at Ciampino military airport in Rome from Paris, she was greeted by crowds of reporters and journalists and photographers surrounding her as she landed. She gave them back as good as they gave her.

"If you are sure I am a sinner," she said, "let whoever is without sin throw the first stone" (a Madonnaesque version of the Bible's "He that is without sin among you, let him first cast a stone at her" [John 8:7]).

Soberly dressed in very non-Madonna black with a string of pearls, she then read a handwritten statement:

"I ask you, fair-minded men and women of the Catholic church—come to see my show and judge it for yourselves. My show is not a conventional rock concert but a theatrical presentation of my music and, like the theater, it poses questions, provokes thought, and takes you on an emotional journey."

Then the paparazzi got into the act and began to close in on her for pictures, with her bodyguards and the police forming phalanxes to keep them away. She was forced to shout, "That's enough!" several times during the delivery of her statement.

And later, in Barcelona, Spain, Madonna's head bodyguard, Marcus Johnson, had to get rough with the Spanish paparazzi. In an encounter with Juan Valganon, a Spanish journalist, he apparently bruised Valganon a bit. Next day Johnson went to the offices of *El Periodica de Cataluna*, the photographer's newspaper, to apologize. The apology was graciously accepted, and the furor blew over.

In Rome, *L'Osservatore Romano*, the vatican newspaper, published a story criticizing Spanish television for broadcasting Madonna's Barcelona concert, pointing out that it violated "good sense, good taste, and decency."

Of the "Blond Ambition" tour overall, the critics were divided. Greg Kot of the *Chicago Tribune* wrote, "She still isn't much of a singer, but she's long past the stage where that even matters. Madonna doesn't come to croon, she sets out to shake us up and send us home smiling. By the sheer force of her personality, Madonna has made questions about her 'talent' irrelevant."

Edna Gunderson of *USA Today* took Madonna and company to task for lip-synching the song "I'm Following You," a duet with Warren Beatty in her *Breathless* album. The fact that Madonna dared to fake a performance was upsetting to the critic. It was not really singing, she wrote.

"It's mime, an alarming move in the hands of trendsetting Madonna, considering the growing use of recorded tracks in concert."

Robert Hilburn of the *Los Angeles Times* pointed out that many performers use flashy sets, eye-opening costumes, and flashy dancers to cover up their own artistic flaws, counting on the cumulative dazzle to overpower the audience. "Madonna—blessed with a marvelous sense of performance—commands the stage as fully when she is surrounded by dancers as when she is sitting alone in a chair."

Jon Pareles, *The New York Times*: "Madonna clearly wants to make a major statement with 'Blond Ambition,' about the malleability of gender conventions and about a woman taking control. But in the past, she has brought a sense of fun to her purposefulness—a light touch that made her a welcome relief from the ponderousness of earnest 1980s rockers. It's fascinating to watch her perfectionism and her iron will at work, but there's not much pleasure in it."

The New York *Daily News*'s Jim Farber wrote that Madonna performed her role in *Dick Tracy* with every bit of the verve, style, and energy she always exhibited—whether on the stage, on video, or on film. "The star puts on a show that has it all, combining theatrics worthy of a top Broadway play with taboo-trashing worthy of the best rock 'n' roll. To anyone who wondered before, this show proves one thing: Madonna is, in every sense of the term, on top."

Joel Selvin, *San Francisco Chronicle*: "She [Madonna] is Ann Margret with a very nasty attitude, a young, white and blond Tina Turner, a singing and dancing Marilyn Monroe, and still entirely herself. She is Madonna, sui generis. . . .

While her music, which, as he put it, was "pleasantly disposable," she managed to purvey enough rhythm and energy to put over her songs—songs that would not be hits in the hands of a less persuasive and skilled performer.

"Personality is the key to her appeal. She has managed to create an image that has held the public's fascination partly because of its constant dramatic changes and partly because of her own no-sweat attitude."

As her friend Steve Bray said about her to a journalist, "This is a woman who is in complete charge of her life. She calls her own shots."

When a technician questioned her during the Tokyo lap of the tour on one of her decisions during a sound check, she replied in typical Madonnaese, "Listen. Everyone is entitled to my opinion."

As proof of her control over herself, at the windup of this, her biggest world tour ever, Madonna in concert was televised by delayed tape from Nice, France, on the Home Box Office network. HBO, owned by Time Warner, paid her a million dollars for the rights. It turned out to be HBO's most-watched nonsports event ever.

20

A Very Good Year

All in all, no one could dispute the fact that 1990 was a very good year for Madonna and company.

ITEM: She opened on the big screen as Breathless Mahoney in Warren Beatty's comic-strip epic *Dick Tracy*.

ITEM: She launched and completed a successful world tour to publicize herself as the epitome of "Blond Ambition."

ITEM: She released an anthology of all her songs in a collection album titled *The Immaculate Collection*.

ITEM: She was named on the December 1990 cover of *Glamour* as one of the Ten Women of the Year "for personifying women's power of self-determination."

ITEM: She was featured in a *Forbes* magazine article with a headline on the cover that read AMERICA'S SMARTEST BUSINESS WOMEN?

The entire citation in *Glamour* is quoted in full:

Once again, this singer/dancer/actress/videatrix/ phenomenon came up with a new persona that delighted and amused some—and shocked others. The 1990 Madonna "Vogued" her way back to the top of the charts (for the nineteenth time) and made us all Breathless when she stole Warren Beatty's stylish *Dick Tracy* by playing an old-style nightclub vamp.

Then she hit the road with a lavish, worldwide concert tour aptly named 'Blond Ambition,' in which she strutted onstage in a pin-striped suit and her chorus boys wore bras. Madonna's energy and imagination upset the stereotypes that have kept women trapped in their cultural roles.

While other media stars come and go, Madonna remains as hot as ever—and we admire her for it. By now, she has become more than a mere celebrity; she has made herself into a blonde, brash, multimillion dollar corporation.

"It's great to be powerful," she told a reporter this year. "I've been striving for it all my life."

In the *Forbes* article, titled "A Brain for Sin and a Bod for Business," it was pointed out that she had earned an estimated $125 million over the past five years and was right up there among the world's highest paid women for the past two years.

As one of her more low-keyed projects for the year, she flew to Paris to prepare a video of a brand-new song, "Justify My Love," a number to be included in *The Immaculate Collection* anthology, with the video scheduled to kick off the album.

By now Madonna had found a new boyfriend, named Tony Ward. She used him in the scenario of the video. To produce the video, she hired Jean-Baptiste Mondino, who had directed the video for her song "Open Your Heart," originally released in 1986.

For "Justify My Love," Madonna opted for a reprise of the black-and-white filming so popular in "Vogue," inasmuch as it was another stylist backward look at the Golden Age of film. The black-and-white photography added both a fantasy look (it was obviously make-believe inasmuch as it was filmed) and a realistic look (inasmuch as it had shades of film noir in its story line).

The cast of characters included a number of people, with the main protagonists Madonna, Ward, and Amanda Cazalet, a twenty-five-year-old Parisian model. The inclusion of this "other" woman in the story line afforded a chance to include just a touch of the kinky.

Mondino assembled the cast of the video in Paris's Royal Monceau Hotel, reportedly locking them all up in the suite for two days in order to prepare them for the shooting. By that time the cast was familiar with the story—and each other—and was beginning to get warmed up for the actual photography.

The action begins with Madonna in a trench coat, entering an unnamed hotel hallway, clutching a suitcase in her hand. She's in black bra, stockings, and stiletto heels—all accentuated by the stylish black-and-white photography. The hallway is obviously the hallway of the psyche, the corridor of the imagination. The scene itself resembles an old-fashioned bordello.

As she moves along, swinging her body to the insinuating beat of the music, she is joined by her boyfriend, a very macho Latin type, with tattoos, well-developed musculature, dark hair and skin, and dressed in casual shirt and slacks. Madonna puts the moves on him as they turn to enter a hotel room.

There are no lyrics. Madonna simply employs an operatic recitative, half-singing and half-saying the words: She does not want to be a mother or a sister. She just wants to be a man's lover.

In the bedroom the two make love—she in a bra and panties and he topless after stripping off his shirt. The love scene is now intercut with fantasies that are racing through her mind. These include a number of scenes suggesting bondage, voyeurism, transvestism, multiple couplings, and lesbian and homosexual embraces.

In one of the intercuts Madonna lip-synchs with the female model Cazalet, who is dressed sleazily as a *Cabaret*-era hooker, wearing suspenders that barely cover her nipples. The fantasies continue, with Madonna, Cazalet, and Ward all offering various types of Kama Sutra techniques.

More intercuts: Two androgynous males pat each other on the bottom. A man is observed standing to the side and watching Madonna and Ward making love. A bare-breasted woman kisses a man, who is seen strapped to a chair in obvious sadomasochistic bondage.

Soon the fantasy expires, the lovemaking is done, and the last scene shows Madonna, carrying her suitcase, walking back down the hallway where she entered, but refreshed, renewed, and giggling at the memory of immediate past pleasures.

On the screen these printed words appear:

POOR IS THE MAN WHOSE PLEASURES
DEPEND ON THE PERMISSION OF ANOTHER.

To be fair, no explicit sexual scenes appear in the video at all. All the images of bondage, voyeurism, transvestism, and multiple couplings are suggestive in the way a dream is suggestive and yet somehow implicit.

To feature the song, MTV, which had grown fat and saucy on Madonna's productions through the years, was scheduling what it called a "Madonnathon"—a long series of Madonna's videos—for the last weekend in November.

Until—

On Monday morning, preceding the Saturday night Madonnathon, MTV executives finally screened the finished version of the Paris video.

"We respect her work as an artist and think she makes great videos," MTV executives said in a joint statement. "This one is not for us."

Thus the "Justify My Love" video was canceled from the celebration of Madonna's forty-eight-hour marathon of videos, concert recordings, film clips, and interviews featuring the star.

Immediately reached in Los Angeles, Madonna explained what her own conception of the video was:

"It's the interior of a human being's mind," she said.

"These fantasies and thoughts exist in every person."

Of course.

She went on, speaking about MTV's decision to cancel the spot.

"Why is it that people are willing to go to a movie and watch someone get blown to bits for no reason and nobody wants to see two girls kissing or two men snuggling? I think the video is romantic and loving and has humor in it."

But she did not blast MTV.

"MTV has been good to me, and they know their audience," she added. "If it's too strong for them, I understand that."

However, by acting in the manner they did, MTV's executives made "MTV look like an organization of aging church elders, and [Madonna] herself a champion of feminism and free expression in the process," according to *Time*.

The New York Times leaped into the fray. Stephen Holden viewed the controversial film. " ' Justify My Love,' in fact, is not as sexually explicit as some of Madonna's onstage exploits during her recent 'Blond Ambition' tour, in which she simulated an autoerotic orgasm. HBO broadcast the concert live from Paris unexpurgated."

In one of Madonna's defenses of her work she told the press, "People would rather deal with death than their own sexuality."

Holden wrote that "Justify My Love" expertly expressed "in sleek video imagery" Madonna's own statement about death and sexuality.

Moments after the announcement of the cancelation of the video, dozens of people not involved in any way with the song or the video had something to say about MTV's option to cancel.

Karen Durbin, arts editor of *Mirabella* magazine, said, "You get all kinds of outrageous stuff on MTV. But on the rare occasions when a woman is in charge and plays around with these same subjects, it gets suppressed. It certainly is absurd of them to come out as sensitive over sadomasochism, when sadomasochism is all that the heavy metal [videos] are anyway. I think the problem is that it's generated by a woman."

Lisa Lewis, author of *Gender Politics and MTV: Voicing the Difference*, put it this way: "MTV is overwhelmingly addressed to male adolescents. MTV is sexist in that it has a history of promoting male musicians and male points of view."

Mark Crispin Miller, a professor of popular culture at Johns Hopkins University, said, "It's perfectly all right for MTV to broadcast sadomasochistic couplings and events as long as the images don't violate a certain heterosexual norm. Madonna must have crossed the boundary line by showing homosexuality."

A Johns Hopkins associate professor of humanities, Judith Butler, author of *Gender Trouble*, said, "It's just like the [Robert] Maplethorpe issue. One of the reasons [homosexuality] has become so threatening is because it's becoming linked up with AIDS. It's a bad climate for sexual experimentation and representations of nontraditional sexuality."

Lewis pointed out that Madonna was seen as threatening by men, but not by women. "Madonna, in order to be as popular as she is, would have to address many ages and all sexes. But she has a very different appeal to girls and women, based on the power she exerts over her image and over female representation in general."

One unnamed observer was quoted by the *Los Angeles Times*'s Patrick Goldstein: "It's a very sexually ambiguous video. You see women you think are men, women with painted-on mustaches. You see Madonna making love with her boyfriend and then kissing another woman, while he watches them.

There were all kinds of fantasy scenes, with people dressed in sadomasochistic gear, even a woman wearing suspenders and nothing else above the waist. Some people would probably call it "wild," the observer admitted.

Because of the news of the cancelation, interest was hyped to the nth degree, and almost immediately various television programs asked for cuts of the video or purchased the entire thing for broadcast.

Entertainment Tonight used sixty seconds of excerpts.
Saturday Night Live used ninety seconds of excerpts.
CNN's *Showbiz Today* used 112 seconds of excerpts.
The *Howard Stern Show* showed the entire video.

Nightline showed the video and featured an interview with Madonna about the brouhaha surrounding it.

The *Nightline* interview, conducted by Forrest Sawyer, rather than Ted Koppel, who was away on assignment, was a fairly disjointed discussion, but Madonna was on hand to answer several questions and state her points of view on some of the sexual problems at the root of the controversy.

Sawyer, who came on like a small-screen version of Tomás de Torquemada, the inquisitor general of the Spanish Inquisition, confronted her with this:

"You certainly were bending the rules a lot more than you had in the past, or did you feel that you were well within the bounds that you had been?"

"I guess half of me thought I was going to get away with it, and that I was going to be able to convince them, and the other half thought, 'Well, no.' "

Sawyer stated his impression that Madonna was "pushing the limits of sexuality," and when Madonna asked him where he thought the line was drawn in general, he wanted her to outline specifically where *she* would draw the line.

"I draw the line in terms of what I think is viewable on television. I draw the line at violence and humiliation and degradation."

Sawyer cited her video "Express Yourself," in which Madonna was at one point seen in chains. "There are images of you crawling under a table, and a lot of people were upset by that."

"I'm chained to myself, though," Madonna retorted. "There wasn't a man that put that chain on me. . . . I was chained to my desires. I crawled under my own table. . . . I'm in charge. . . . Degradation is when somebody else is making you do something against your wishes."

Later she said, "If we're going to have censorship, let's not be hypocrites about this. Let's not have double standards. . . . Why is it okay for ten-year-olds to see someone's body being ripped to shreds or Sam Kenison spitting on Jessica Hahn? . . . Why do parents not have a problem with that, but . . . have a problem with two adults, two consenting adults, displaying affection for each other, regardless of their sex?"

Sawyer responded: "When a ten-year-old sees you chained

to the bed or sees your boyfriend bound up and another woman comes by while you're there . . . [that] ten-year-old's going to get awfully confused."

"Good," Madonna said. "Let them get confused and let them go ask their parents about it and let their parents explain to them that it is a sexual fantasy and that these things exist in life."

Sawyer suggested that some feminists didn't like Madonna and her interpretations of women and sex because of the BOY TOY belt buckle and the way she dressed.

"I would like to point out that they're missing a couple of things. . . . I may be dressing like the typical bimbo or whatever, but I'm in charge. I'm in charge of my fantasies."

Sawyer wondered how Madonna would feel about exposing sexuality on television if she were the parent of a ten- or eleven-year-old. "Would you not be worried about their seeing this kind of stuff?"

"Personally," she replied, "I wouldn't be worried about it, and this is why. Because I think that sexuality is something that Americans would really rather just sweep under the rug. And I think that if my video provokes an open discussion, maybe kids will go and ask their parents these questions. If it provokes an open discussion about sex with their parents, I think this is a really good thing."

The results of the interview? *Nightline* got its biggest ratings share of the year! Even the channels that used only part of the video raised or exceeded their highest ratings of the week.

Was there a lesson in all this?

The *Wall Street Journal*'s Robert Goldberg watched the video and after thinking about it, discussed portions of the song, the concept, and the overall content.

"And the song? Well, there is no song to 'Justify My Love.' " Madonna says that she's yearning. Pause. She's burning. Pause. She's waiting. "You'll wait a long time for any kind of *tune* to start," Goldberg wrote, equating the song itself to a lengthy spoken introduction before a main song kicks into gear—except that in this case there never *is* a main lyrical song. Only a few sighed words.

"So is the whole thing sexy? Well, kind of. But as a video

and as a song, 'Justify My Love' is really only one long come-on, a tease that beckons and beckons and never delivers any satisfaction in the end."

In the end Madonna won the whole affair hands down.

With "Justify My Love" banned from MTV, she and Warner Bros. decided to retail it as a new video single at $9.98. As such it would be the first video single ever released. Ten dollars usually bought a three-song video.

This meant that five minutes of "Justify My Love" would cost the buyer two dollars a minute!

It was MTV that actually made it possible for this first-time video to be released as a single.

No wonder Madonna said, "MTV has been good to me."

This was not, however, to be the end of "Justify My Love." On one of the versions of the song released in the single—there were five versions, called remixes—trouble reared its ugly head once again. This time in the form of racism.

In what came to be known as "The Beast Within Mix," Madonna read a passage from the Bible, little thinking that it could stir up as much controversy as—well, as from *not* reading the Bible. She chose several paragraphs from the Book of Revelation, in which John sees an apocalyptic vision of Judgment Day.

In the King James Version the words are:

> 8 And unto the angel of the church in Smyrna write; These things saith the first and the last, which was dead, and is alive.
>
> 9 I know thy works, and tribulation, and poverty, (but thou art rich) and I *know* the blasphemy of them which say they are Jews, and are not, but *are* the synagogue of Satan.
>
> 10 Fear none of those things which thou shalt suffer: behold, the devil shall cast *some* of you into prison, that ye may be tried; and ye shall have tribulation ten days: be thou faithful unto death, and I will give thee a crown of life.

(Incidentally the version Madonna read was not the King James Version but a more modern translation. Her words in the key section went, "I know your tribulation and poverty, and the slander of those who say that they are Jews, but they are not, they are a synagogue of Satan.")

Almost simultaneous with the release of the remix came the repercussions—from Rabbi Abraham Cooper, of the Simon Weisenthal Center—accusing her of indulging in anti-Semitism. He cited the passage above as "one of the most notorious anti-Semitic quotes in the New Testament."

A stunned Madonna fired a letter right back at him. "People can say I am an exhibitionist, but no one can ever accuse me of being a racist," she said. "I am not even going to try to defend myself against such ridiculous accusations."

And she wrote, "I certainly didn't have any anti-Semitic intent when I included a passage from the Bible on my record. My message, if any, is pro-tolerance and anti-hate. The song is, after all, about love."

Cooper said, "We acknowledge from the outset that this passage comes right from the New Testament, but that in itself is no excuse. Quoting bigoted remarks from the Bible only serves to fuel the doctrine of anti-Semitism preached by a growing number of white supremicists, including the Christian-identity movement."

Rabbi Cooper was disturbed by the lyrics, although he recognized Madonna's honest concern. "She was direct to the issue, she responded quickly and we're relieved that she did so. You don't need to be a sociologist to know that racism is alive and well in America."

Cooper made another point: "We believe that the First Amendment rights have to be balanced with responsibility. This is not the kind of thing that should warrant congressional hearings or reverends or rabbis starting boycotts. The music industry understands that this kind of offensive terminology is wrong and should be deleted."

An antipornography crusader in Florida named Jack Thompson, a born-again Christian activist engaged in a campaign to halt the sale of the same record, but for very different reasons, took a quite different stand:

"All Madonna's doing here is reading Scripture written by Jews about a Jewish messiah," he said. "Rabbi Cooper's problem seems not to be with Madonna but with the Jewish

Jesus, and the way I see it, he better figure out who Jesus is before what John is writing about happens. My problem with Madonna isn't what she relates from the Bible, it's what she relates from *Hustler* magazine to the small children who worship her."

In a reflection of Cooper's fears of racism, Abraham Foxman, national director of the Anti-Defamation League of B'nai B'rith, protested the use of the biblical quotation in "The Beast Within Mix" of "Justify My Love" in a letter to Lenny Waronker, president of Warner Bros. Records: "It may be more than a coincidence that within days of the release of 'Justify My Love,' three synagogues and a high school in Ventura County, California, were vandalized with anti-Semitic graffiti referring to Revelation 2:9."

Sholom Comay, president of the American Jewish Committee, also wrote Madonna. "Even though the language you sang was taken from biblical sources, it was taken out of context. The larger real-world context is that Jews for centuries have been victims of prejudice and murder 'justified' by misapplied biblical passages.

"Today, the only people who use the 'Jew as Satan' image are those whose message is not about love but about bone-chilling hate."

In spite of her steely resolve not to let negative publicity and personal attacks get under her skin, the controversy over "Justify My Love" *did* irritate her.

"This year I couldn't do *anything* to stay out of trouble," she said about 1990. "I know I like to provoke, but this year has been like a train out of control."

The train may have been out of control, but it resulted in a record-breaking run. She got huge exposure out of it, and even huger profits.

Seymour Stein, president of Sire, her record company, put it neatly: "Madonna can turn catastrophes into triumphs." He admitted that when he first viewed "Justify My Love" he groaned aloud. He *knew* it would be a problem. "But it's turned out to be the biggest-selling video of its type!"

Madonna was philosophical about her out-of-control year. "I wish I hadn't done a lot of things, but, on the other hand, if I hadn't, I wouldn't be here."

Still, the fear of inevitable inadequacy continued to gnaw at her. "All of my will has always been to conquer some horrible feeling of inadequacy. I'm always struggling with that fear. I push past one spell of it and discover myself as a special human being and then I get to another stage and think I'm mediocre and uninteresting."

Her drive in life, she said, always came from this horrible fear of being mediocre. "Even though I've become Somebody, I still have to prove that I'm *Somebody*. My struggle has never ended, and it probably never will."

In addition to mediocrity, she has been forced to endure the gut-wrenching loneliness of the long-distance runner. "I long for children," she told *Vanity Fair*. "I wish that I was married and in a situation where having a child would be possible."

Friends kept telling her, "Well, have one on your own."

To which Madonna usually responded, "Wait a minute. I'm not interested in raising a cripple. I want a father there. I want someone I can depend on."

About a solid relationship, she once said, "I can think of isolated moments where I could have given in and it would have made things better. But, all in all, I'm not with any of the people I'm not with for a much larger reason: we just weren't meant to be. If I had changed and given in, or what I conceived to be giving in, to certain concessions that people had asked of me, maybe the relationships would have been successful on the one hand, but then I would have had to give up other things in my career. And then I would have been miserable." No question about that.

"I'm not exactly sure who I'm looking for," Madonna said. "I wish I knew. I wonder if I could ever find someone like me."

Laughter.

"If I did, I would probably kill them."

We have met the enemy, and they is us.

The guy she was looking for turned out not to be Tony Ward, even though she might well have thought it was during the making of the "Justify My Love" video.

Whatever happened to old Tony? her friends began to wonder.

It was a very simple thing. Prior to meeting Madonna and working with her, Tony Ward had married a woman named Amalia Papadimos, an Australian who had emigrated from Greece; Ward married her in Las Vegas.

"I married him because I loved him," Amalia told reporters later. "It's as simple as that—and I didn't do it to get a green card to be able to stay and work in America. What you've got to remember is that I had been going out with Tony for twelve months, and we were very much in love. I even planned to take him back to Australia on our honeymoon and introduce him to my parents."

It didn't work out that way. Tony met Madonna and worked with her until she discovered he was already married. When she found that out she simply dumped him. Dalliance with a married man was not for Madonna; her scruples might be different from those of others, but she had a fine-tuned set of them.

Where Tony and Amalia went after the abrupt rupture is anybody's guess. As for Madonna, it was not a case of *"arrividerci, Antonio,"* but simply "good-bye forever."

The old problem of the nudie pictures of Madonna—those that were displayed worldwide on the eve of Madonna's wedding to Sean Penn—was still alive in 1991, and the pictures were doing quite well indeed. Martin Schreiber, one of the art-class teachers who had taken nude studies of the fledgling celebrity after she had signed all the proper releases, found himself in a lucrative business position as he continued to peddle naked Madonnas.

After selling the photos to *Playboy* during the sudden divestiture of Madonna in 1985, he had developed a new marketing ploy: "platinum prints." Eleven nude platinum prints of Madonna were on sale—and for only nine thousand dollars! Exclusively issued in only twenty-five sets, each set came with a pair of cotton gloves—because the prints were too delicate to be touched by human hands, don't you see?

Besides this pitch, Schreiber also offered limited editions of sixteen-by-twenty photos of Madonna for only nine hundred dollars each—obviously a steal. In addition to these goodies, Schreiber also peddled Madonna posters and books.

21
High Priestess of Hype

In the winter of 1988–89 a young Harvard graduate named Alek Keshishian showed a film of a pop-opera version of Emily Brontë's novel *Wuthering Heights*, which he had made for his doctoral thesis, to Creative Artists Agency, the theatrical agent who represented him *and* Madonna—and who in turn screened it for Madonna.

It was an interesting work, with the performers lip-synching a score consisting of professionally made contemporary pop records—including some of Madonna's. Keshishian started out with the voice of Kate Bush as Cathy in the novel, which eventually turned into the voice of Madonna—delineating the change from the Gothic's heroine to the twentieth-century pop icon Madonna.

Sufficiently impressed, Madonna asked Keshishian for an interview. At the time, he had just finished directing a music video—his first—titled "Don't Be Cruel" for Bobby Brown, then an unknown. Although the Madonna interview progressed favorably, nothing came of it—for the time being.

It was, in fact, not until March 1990 that Madonna finally thought of Keshishian again. After the Nike-commercial deal blew up in her face and Nike's competitor, Reebok, started playing games with her, she found she had grown gun-shy about advertising moguls and decided to get financial backing from some other source.

One such source might be a film version of her upcoming Blond Ambition tour. Thinking of that, she remembered her interview with the young Harvard graduate.

As Keshishian tells the story, he was at his computer in L.A. doping out some video treatments when the phone rang.

"Hi, Alek, it's Madonna," the voice said. "I don't know if you've heard, but I'm about to go on world tour, and I was wondering if you'd like to film it."

Two days later in the Disney Studios they were working out the plan in its bare-bones outline: photograph the production numbers, splice together the best parts of the best, add some backstage "insider" stuff, and create a theatrical exhibition motion picture.

Backing the venture with four million dollars of her own money, Madonna made the deal with Keshishian, and soon he and two crews of three each were on their way with the enormous troupe of dancers, singers, and musicians.

After shooting their stormy opening in Japan, Keshishian and his crew began looking at the film they had shot and puzzling over it. It was all there—in fact, it was more than *all* there. It was something else again.

"As I looked at the backstage footage," Keshishian recalled later, "I became incredibly excited. This world was very Felliniesque. The dancers were accessible and flamboyant, and Madonna was like the matriarch in a circus. There was an odd connection among the people because almost everybody came from a broken home or from an unusual family."

Keshishian went to Madonna with a new concept: increase the percentage of the backstage stuff and let it run parallel to the production numbers. Madonna referred him to her advisers, who hashed it all over. Definitely no, was the consensus. Cinema verité documentaries had proved absolutely and totally failure-prone in the past. Four million dollars was too much money to risk on a flop—particularly when it was Madonna's own money. And, additionally, since no one knew if the damned tour itself would pay off. It was not no, but *hell* no.

And then came the revisionist meetings. Well, maybe yes. It was Madonna who weighed the backing and filling of her advisers, saw her own vision of what could be, and decided to go flat-out ahead.

"Madonna," Keshishian said, "I'm going to film you in the morning with your breakfast room service, and at night I'll be waiting for you in the shower."

The candid stuff started immediately. The backstage material was done in hand-held 16-mm black-and-white, the production material in widescreen color. The hand-held 16-mm crew dogged her determinedly. Every moment.

Madonna did not want *that*.

"Initially she fought me," Keshishian said, referring to the backstage shooting. "She would do one of two things. She would run ahead of the camera while we were following her with this big heavy equipment, say she was having a business meeting, and shut the door in our faces. Or else I would be filming and she would tell me to stop filming, in which case I would keep filming anyway."

And so a cat-and-mouse game developed. Within the four and a half months of the exhausting worldwide tour, Keshishian and his crews filmed 250 hours of film.

By the time the tour ended on the Riviera, with a worldwide telecast of the show itself, Keshishian had not only the key elements of the production itself on film, but a staggering number of personal interviews, candid scenes, conversations, and sequences for use.

And then came the formidable task of putting it all together into a viable documentary.

It would have to be a foolish individual who did not guess that something was in the wind when once again Madonna seemed to be appearing everywhere all at once. This time the publicity hype itself began with a tease interview in *Vanity Fair* with a bit of predocumentary mention, spread to the usual national mags like *Time* and *Newsweek* with news of the documentary, and for a capper, *The Advocate*, a magazine for homosexuals, and *everybody* with clips of the show in hand. Almost on cue Madonna began appearing on television everywhere one tuned in.

By the time the documentary itself was previewed in Los

Angeles on Monday, May 16, 1991, even people who knew all about it wanted to see it anyway.

The documentary is titled almost unbelievably *Truth or Dare: On the Road, Behind the Scenes, and in Bed with Madonna.*

This is a two-tiered production. The first tier is what is shot in color, soundtracked with scores of tapes booming out from every part of the theater, featuring long shots of dancers, close-ups of Madonna; it abounds in movement, bright lights, and the constant and unsettling booming of the base drums and other rhythmic elaborations.

The second tier—the sophisticated viewer's tier—is what is shot in old-fashioned black-and-white, filmed in home-movie casual style, revealing the intimate backstage life that only insiders in theater are supposed to know.

There is a tremendous drive to the production that manages to carry all opposition before it. And the black-and-white overview of the color story tends to give the totality an added dimension that the simple screening of the dances and songs would not provide. In the end one knows more about Madonna than one has known before; but this in turn accounts for a puzzling realization that perhaps one knows more about Madonna than Madonna knows about herself.

The picture that emerges is of a more or less perplexed individual who, in spite of being an international star the magnitude of which has never been equaled or even approached before, does not really have control of herself, her persona, or her inner frustrations and needs. And who is still trying to puzzle herself out.

One of the most poignant of the black-and-white cutaways—the structure of the production involves a hurtling onward-and-upward progression of production numbers intercut with black-and-white backstage commentary—shows us a backstage visit of Madonna's father and stepmother. This is preceded by an intimate close-up of Madonna on the telephone chatting with her father, asking him a simple question that he seems unable to answer: How many tickets to the show does he want?

There is always at the back of the mind a tickle of unutterable suspense; maybe her father doesn't *want* to see the show!

But no. However the scene ends—we don't know because at the end of the phone call no decision has been made—he apparently does specify a number of tickets and the time he will come. Suspense is underlined by the odd staging of the telephone scene. Madonna is typically earring-removed-glued to the handset, but what seems to be the focal point of the scene is a huge round feeding bowl from which Madonna continues to scoop enormous globs of foodstuff—its identity is never clear—as she chomps down sustenance during the conversation.

She warns her father that perhaps he doesn't really want to come at all but he insists that he does—then asks her if there is a lot of—well, *you* know. If there is, he suggests, too much—of *that*—she should tone it down for him. No, disagrees Madonna. If she did that, she would be unfaithful to her artistic integrity. Oh, sure.

In the backstage visit itself, father and daughter discuss almost nothing about the content of the show. In due time Madonna excuses herself; she's got to change. Obviously, she does not want her father to see her in her underwear. Why not? we wonder. The entire world has seen her in her underwear—so have we—and less. Nevertheless, she excuses herself and *does* change in front of the camera. And, for a split second, she *is* frontally nude—the only split second in the show that *anyone* female is frontally nude.

Asked later what her father thought of the show, Madonna reports that he thought it was just a bit burlesquey, but that he liked it.

"Do you think your mother would have objected?"

"My mother would have *loved* it!"

One behind-the-scenes revelation features the somewhat dramatic confrontation between Madonna's producer—or perhaps lawyer or manager—and the Toronto, Canada, police. If Madonna insists on using her masturbation number onstage—the famous "Like a Virgin" reprise—the Toronto police have been authorized to shut down production. In the end it's a standoff; Madonna refuses to alter the content of the show, citing artistic integrity again, but it's all left in the air anyway.

The number goes on. Nothing happens. Eventually the

Toronto police inform Madonna that they were going to view the show only to see if it was obscene; they did, it wasn't, they left.

Publicity, publicity.

One of the best backstage sequences involves the presence of Warren Beatty during an eye, ear, nose, and throat examination of Madonna's larynx. She is hoarse and wants medication. There is a great deal of "ahing," "ughing," and "ohing," with Beatty pictured looking on, dressed in his usual dark glasses inside the dimly lit dressing room, with a kind of intergalactic amusement on his face.

"The insanity of doing this on film," he muses at one point. "This *insane* atmosphere!"

After spraying her throat with gallons of ointment, the doctor watches Madonna move to another part of the dressing room, and asks her if she wants to say anything off-camera. She just shakes her head.

Beatty snaps, "She doesn't talk unless she's on-camera." In fact, Beatty goes on, playing with the idea, she doesn't *do* anything when she's off-camera. "She doesn't want to *live* off-camera. What point is there to existing?"

Her life, Beatty means, is *being* on-camera.

There's actually no mystery to the documentary's somewhat puzzling title.

"The idea of Truth or Dare is a joke," Madonna explained later. "It's like all those childhood games. I dare you to do this. . . . If everybody put on film what they did in those games when they were children or their fraternity games, I mean, my God, they'd all be arrested.

"The dancers used to play it all the time in the beginning [of the tour]. I was never really part of it. The point of it is to relieve boredom, fuck with people. It's great for relieving tensions and animosities. Or if someone has a crush on somebody and the other person wants to find out. In the guise of a game you can find these things out. Sometimes it would turn into those really heavy sessions where it was all truths and no dares. Did you really do this? Were you sleeping with so-and-so? Everyone gets their feelings out and then after you've played the game everyone is closer. That's the theory. It's like group therapy."

In one "dare" sequence, Madonna forces one of her black dancers to expose his penis to the assembled crowd. With the hand-held 16-mm film, *we* don't see anything, but she does.

"I swear to God—it's purple!" she shrieks.

In another short take, Madonna discusses her family with Sandra Bernhard, remembering that after her mother died, Madonna would be unable to sleep at night without recurring nightmares: Hands would reach up from the ground, grasping at her, hands of the dead, of course. She'd jump out of bed and crawl in with her father.

Bernhard looks at her in surprise. "And then what?"

"Nothing!" cries Madonna. But she cannot refrain from being Madonna. "After he fucked me!" she giggles, then puts up her hand: "Just kidding!"

The two then engage in a little sex gossip.

MADONNA: Are you sleeping with her?
SANDRA: I hate her.
MADONNA: I hate everybody I sleep with.
SANDRA (wisely): That's why you sleep with them.

After a bit more give-and-take, Sandra sizes up Madonna.

SANDRA: Who in the world *would* you most like to meet?
MADONNA (with megastar weltschmerz): I don't know. I think I've met everybody.

There is even a scene in which Madonna's brother Martin is shown trying to pick up one of the backup singers in the crowded backstage. It is revealed that he has just been released from an alcohol rehabilitation center. He promises to return that night to talk to Madonna, but he never shows up. The camera pursues her as she reappears again and again, looking for him; finally she shrugs and locks the door. He's stood her up.

"It's obvious I was upset because I thought that he'd missed coming to see me because he'd stopped to get something to drink," Madonna told a journalist later. "And when you see footage of him trying to explain it, it's obvious that it's a con job. But I also think that he's very entertaining. My brother is a ham. He's an exhibitionist. And he knew full well what he was doing."

She added: "He's very tortured" and "is a very hard person to get along with. He's an elusive, enigmatic character. He's very charming but, yes, he is an alcoholic. . . . We have a strained relationship."

The much-publicized Kevin Costner incident occurs during a swirl of backstage activity. "What do you think of the show?" Madonna asks him.

Costner thinks a moment. "Neat," he says with a complimentary smile.

As Costner drifts away, Madonna goes into a quick burn. "Neat!" she rages. "Anybody who says my show is 'neat' *has* to go!" Then, to make the point inescapable, she pokes her forefinger down into her throat to simulate deliberate gagging—pantomiming the ancient George S. Kaufman–Moss Hart line from *The Man Who Came to Dinner:* "I may vomit."

One segment focuses on a conversation between Madonna and a childhood girlfriend, Moira McFarland. In its own way it is poignant and disturbing in its revelation of what incredible damage fame and fortune can do to any personal relationship.

According to Keshishian, the meeting was his idea and his alone—one he "manipulated" for the documentary.

During the first part of the tour, he heard Madonna talk about one of her childhood friends with affection. Once back in the States from Japan, Keshishian looked up Moira McFarland, who had become a housewife and mother in North Carolina, and introduced himself to her. When Madonna's troupe hit Washington, D.C., Keshishian had Moira driven into town and, without telling Madonna, stationed her in the hotel so that she would "accidentally" encounter her in full view of the cameras.

The meeting is painful. Moira is hoping for a friendly encounter; she brings a painting to present to Madonna, and asks Madonna why she hasn't answered her letters. Madonna is distant, but friendly. Then she begins to reminisce about her youth with Moira, saying that it was Moira who taught her how to stuff her bra, to insert a tampon, to French kiss, and, indeed, was the person who introduced Madonna to sex when she "finger-fucked" her in bed one night.

The expression on the poor woman's face is absolutely riveting. She has since confessed to *People* magazine that she has no recollection whatever of this incident. When this exchange between the two shows signs of petering out, Moira confesses that she is pregnant again and asks Madonna to be the godmother of her child. Stunned, Madonna does not answer. She says she'll let Moira know.

MOIRA: Good-bye, Madonna.
MADONNA: Good-bye, Moira.
MOIRA (under her breath): You little shit!

A few moments later, Madonna is disparaging the gift painting to her backstage associates.

"She was still really a stranger, in a lot of ways," Madonna confessed later. "What was really weird was that here was this girl that I idolized from my childhood. I really thought she was the cat's pajamas, you know? Then it was like, 'Look what's happened to our lives.' The juxtaposition of how I went that way and she went that way and we both came from the exact same place."

Madonna admitted: "She's had that baby. I'm not the godmother. But I have written to her a couple of times. I was touched that she asked me to be the godmother, but I don't have the time to fly to North Carolina and participate in this whole ritual."

Keshishian's scene manipulation pays off here. But in another scene—the scene in which Madonna visits her mother's grave—Keshishian swears that there was absolutely *no* manipulation. The director had hidden cameras belowground and in the trees near the grave site. Madonna did not know about them. What she did she did ad libitum.

The scene itself is so riveting it tends to *appear* rigged, for Madonna simply lies down on the ground next to the grave and communes in her own way with the spirit of her mother.

"That's the one place where it's such a private moment that the sheer act of capturing it on camera is going to give you that sense," Keshishian said later. "When that graveyard scene was [finished], I was in the car with her, and she was very moved. It was an exorcism for her. And no matter what anyone says, I think there are glimmers of truth, and loneliness there. It might have been more emotional if the cameras hadn't been there; it might've been less. All I can tell you is that it was emotional for me watching it, there behind the tree."

As for Madonna, "I still cry when I watch that. . . . The single most . . . greatest event in my life [was] my mother dying. . . . I know if I'd had a mother I would be very different [now]. It gave me a lot of what are traditionally looked upon as masculine traits in terms of my ambitiousness and my aggressiveness. Mothers, I think, teach you manners and gentleness and a certain kind of . . . what's the word? . . . patience."

There's an amusing interlude with Madonna reading out a couple of pages of poetic doggerel to honor her assistant on her birthday. The verse is light and funny, with word twists even Ogden Nash wouldn't sneer at. And it ends with a string of obscenities—but Madonna gives it a good reading.

The sleaziest scene of all takes place during a "dare" sequence when Madonna is commanded to perform fellatio on a bottle of Vichy water. She does it, as the cast about her cheers her on with their own unprintable comments.

After viewing the film, Adrian Deevoy, a British journalist, asked her if her father might not find it shocking to see her fellate a bottle. "Is it shocking?"

"Is *what* shocking?" she snapped. "My giving head to a bottle? Why? You see people doing it in movies all the time. It's a joke. What's shocking? Why don't you know if it's shocking or not? Don't you know your own feelings?"

Deevoy riposted with a bit of wordplay. "Do people want this sort of thing rammed down their throats?"

"It's a joke!" Madonna shouted, missing the—uh—gag. But of course the truth was that Madonna had avoided answering the question about the segment's shock value by simply raging away at Deevoy.

In another sequence, Madonna dares two male homosexuals to French kiss, and was later asked what she was thinking as she watched the two gay men going at it.

"What was I *thinking?* My God, well, I think it's incredibly erotic to watch people kiss. For me it was a big turn-on to watch men kiss because you so rarely see it. It's considered to be such a bad thing in society, but I thought it was beautiful."

Next question.

Before each performance, Madonna and the entire cast hold a prayer session, in which they form a circle and hold hands as Madonna intones a prayer out loud to bless the performance and—somehow—help her get her voice back. She was asked if this was a mandatory consideration before every performance, and she said that it *was*.

One thing that the production numbers in *Truth or Dare* illuminate is the intensity of the dancers and their movements. With swift intercuts from one angle to another the viewer is given a real up-front vision of the performers—particularly Madonna. Her white skin is translucent in the bright lights. She is bathed in a sheen of glistening perspiration—today's ultimate stimulator to erotic foreplay, if the sight of sweat-stained workout pullovers ubiquitous on televisioin screens is any indication.

The surface patina of her flesh, moist and glistering, followed so raptly by the camera lenses, gives a tremendous whomp to the sexuality implied by all her moves and countermoves. In their case, the tricky cutting and intercutting of the sensuous travels of Madonna's hands over her own body parts magnifies the erotic implications suggested with never the *need* for her to touch flesh.

Even after the cast crawls are through and the screen is black and the audience is sweeping out of the theater, we are invited to attend a mixed sleepover conversation replete with four-letter words and jocular ripostes about "farts" and having to pee. Probably a live sorority bull session at midnight would be more entertaining—but in this extravaganza it's bigger than life.

Janet Maslin, *The New York Times: "Truth or Dare* is at the very least a potent conversation piece. It can also be seen as a clever, brazen, spirited self-portrait, an ingeniously contrived extension of Madonna's public personality and a studied glimpse into what, in the case of most other pop luminaries, would be at least a quasi-hidden realm. In the case of Madonna, who is even filmed gossiping in the rest room and visiting her mother's grave, no such sacrosanct territory is shown to exist. Nothing is too private for Madonna to flaunt in public."

Don Shewey, *The Advocate:* "You ain't seen nothin' . . . until you've seen *Truth or Dare*, [Madonna's] documentary film. . . . Salacious tidbits from the film shot during the Blond Ambition tour have been conversation pieces for weeks: Here's Madonna reminiscing about the childhood girlfriend who finger-fucked her, there's Madonna bluntly asking one of her dancers if he's ever taken it up the ass and then watching openmouthed while two others act out her dare to tongue-kiss each other."

Steve Dougherty et al., *People:* "[*Truth or Dare*] is a startling, frank portrayal of a woman who may be more entertaining—and more temperamental, and cruder—offstage than on. The language ain't for the fainthearted: Watching the male dancers kiss, Madonna yelps: 'Oh, God! I'm getting a hard-on!' Sitting backstage and picking petals off a daisy, she muses, 'He loves me. He loves me not. He just wants to fuck me.' "

James Kaplan, *Entertainment:* "Her power can't be denied; only her artistic intent is puzzling. By applying her image-making skills to what appears to be her actual life, she has passed some point of no return and moved into anxious new territory: How after this, could she ever give us less? . . . In the nine months since her tour ended, Madonna has brought the state of her art—whatever it is—to a new level. She's found her true medium at last: This is her greatest, her only, role."

Adrian Deevoy, *Q* [London]: "*Truth or Dare* throws up a lot of questions about Madonna: from her motives to her ethics, from the credibility of her public persona to the accessibility of her private parts."

They showed *Truth or Dare* at the Forty-fourth Cannes Film Festival during the main part of the screenings, but specifically out of the competition. Vincent Canby of *The New York Times* pointed out that the showing was the week's second-hardest ticket to come by, the hardest being a ticket to Madonna's party in celebration of it!

"Priorities tend to get confused when Madonna is around," he wrote. "She's not yet a cinema icon; she's a vibrant new public personality who creates the kind of excitement that helps moviemakers survive."

It was Canby's *Times* colleague who had the definitive statement on the not-quite-yet icon:

Stephen Holden, *The New York Times:* "*Truth or Dare* takes a standard movie genre—the rock-tour documentary—and turns it inside out. Although the movie, which is rated R, contains vivid concert footage, including the racy sex-goddess-and-eunuchs staging of 'Like a Virgin,' in which Madonna simulates masturbation, there is every bit as much drama behind the scenes as on stage. . . . In *Truth or Dare*, perhaps for the first time in a film . . . self-consciousness does not impede Madonna's self-expression. The one quality it reveals more than any of her previous work is her sense of humor."

That is precisely the magic phrase—sense of humor.

The high priestess of hype has worked hard at putting her life on film—it only cost four million bucks, she's got plenty more than that, and look what this docu is going to bring in! But she's worked even harder to publicize it. Flying journalists from all over the world to her lofty, sky-high Beverly Hills/Hollywood Hills mansion to screen her story for them and then personally answering questions is a daunting project at best!

And then, once the hype is in print, appearing—well, *everywhere*—on television, sometimes competing with herself to flog the film, is simply frosting on an already oversweetened cake.

Nevertheless, throughout all the long-distance race, the key quality that glowed from within her personality, through all the muck and the mire and the dross—her sense of humor—never ever deserted her.

One example. For the road.

After a long, sometimes tedious verbal Ping-Pong match with Regis Philbin, staged on a sixteenth-floor balcony of the Four Seasons Hotel overlooking smog-ridden Los Angeles,

Philbin and she jousted verbally, tossing quips at one another
until Philbin threw back his head and laughed heartily.

> REGIS: I *love* just being with you!
> MADONNA (instantly): Who doesn't?

22

THE NAKED MADONNA

The compleat Madonna
—including the uninhibited exterior, the flaunting, seductive
persona, and especially the elusive, unpredictable sense of
humor—emerges full-fledged, as can be seen, in her documentary. Yet in spite of all the hype, there *is* a private Madonna, an inner reality that transcends the programmed
celebrity everyone sees.

More than any other superstar today, she has been interviewed so much that her overall views tend to be at one time
slightly north by northwest, at another north by northeast,
and at another maybe south by southwest, deviating from true
north as she views life somewhat differently from day to day.
The subjects Madonna has discussed for the public prints are
incredibly wide-ranging. Yet in a way they become more and
more frank and revelatory as they zero in on her real self.

It is as if Madonna secretly wished to present her psyche
as much in the nude as she has already presented most of her
body—but in a cryptic, enigmatic way. There is nothing rigged,
presorted, or cosmeticized about her verbalizations.

Her natural spontaneity makes her remarks all the more
viable. After interviewing her for *Rolling Stone* magazine, Carrie Fisher said that she felt the secret of Madonna's quotability

was the fact that she would answer any question "because she is genuinely interested in her own reply."

In the following collation of opinions, smatterings of intuition, and bits and tatters of prejudices and judgments, one can glimpse the real Madonna through a haze of words, words, words. Yet somehow "The Naked Madonna" emerges, completely stripped, completely uninhibited, completely frank, completely vulnerable, a somehow haunting icon of the best and the worst of the admittedly American-oriented twentieth century now ending with a bang *and* a whimper—the bang and whimper she herself helped mold and shape.

MADONNA ON ACTING IN A WOODY ALLEN MOVIE:

"To me, the whole process of being a brushstroke in someone else's painting is a little difficult. I'm used to being in charge of everything. So on this movie it's hard for me to shut up and do my job and, well, okay, I have this stupid little part and I have to sit around on the set and wait all day and then say a few lines and blah, blah, blah. . . .

"I can feel all the grips and electricians looking at me— I'm painfully aware of it. They don't see me as an actress, they see me as an icon, and it makes me extremely exhausted."

MADONNA ON ALCOHOLISM:

"My father wasn't an alcoholic, but his parents were. And some of the people in my mother's family are alcoholics. . . . I guess some people would say that my father's behavior was alcoholic behavior. . . . My father didn't give me advice, he just gave orders."

MADONNA OF BEING CONTROVERSIAL:

It's not something I sit around and think about. It's rather unconscious. I just sort of naturally say things to shock, not necessarily to offend. It's like pulling the tablecloth off the table to disarm everybody."

MADONNA ON BEING FIVE FEET FOUR AND A HALF:

"Short people try harder."

MADONNA ON BEING A MAN:

"When I was a little girl, I was insanely jealous of my older brothers. They didn't have curfews, they could pee standing up, they could take their shirts off in the summer, they got to do outdoor work, while we had to do the indoor work. They had so much more freedom and I would just mope about that. And mope and mope and mope about how I wished I was a boy. And then when I was in the ballet world I went through another period where I wished I was a boy because I just wanted *somebody* to ask me out on a date. . . .

"Actually it would be great to be both sexes. Effeminate men intrigue me more than anything in the world. I see them as my alter egos. I feel very drawn to them. I think like a guy, but I'm feminine. So I relate to feminine men."

MADONNA ON BEING SPANKED:

"I despise being spanked. . . . I say I want to be spanked, but it's like, 'Try it and I'll knock your fucking head off.' It's a joke! . . . The spanking thing started because I believed that my character in *Dick Tracy* liked to get smacked around and that's why she hung around with people like Al Pacino's character.

"Warren [Beatty] asked me to write some songs, and one of them—the hanky-panky song—was about that. I say in the song, 'Nothing like a good spanky,' and in the middle I say, 'Ooh, my bottom hurts just thinking about it.' When [the movie] came out, everybody started asking, 'Do you like to get spanked?' and I said, 'Yeah. Yeah, I do.' "

MADONNA ON BUSINESS CONFERENCES:

"I love meetings with suits. I *live* for meetings with suits. I love them because I know they had a really boring week and

I walk in there with my orange velvet leggings and drop popcorn in my cleavage and then fish it out and eat it. I like that. I know I'm entertaining them and I know that they know. Obviously, the best meetings are with suits that are intelligent, because then things are operating on a whole other level."

MADONNA ON CONDOMS:

"They're a drag. Such a *drag*. They interrupt *everything*. It's like, 'Wait a second, wait a second. Do you have a rubber?' 'I think I've left them in my coat!' Aaargh! Then, the worst thing, they say no! And it's 'Oh God! Well . . . well *now what!*' And then it's 'Well, sorry.'

"You know, the best people of them all are the ones who just have them, they are thinking and aware enough to have them. Preferably within easy reach but just to have them tells you a lot about somebody. But you'd be surprised how many men don't carry them. Very surprised. There are a lot of stupid men and the thought just doesn't occur to them because apparently a lot of women don't demand that they wear them. They're not great but they make sense. They've saved *my* life."

MADONNA ON DEATH:

"I was thinking about dying the other day. . . . The death thought came while I was sitting on my toilet peeing—that's where I have my most contemplative moments. . . . I'm obsessed with [dying] because my mother died of breast cancer when she was thirty. . . .

"I go to the mammogram vault on a regular basis. It's the most horrifying thing in the world. You go in and you feel like you're getting your death sentence. First of all it's painful because they smash your breasts into this thing. Then you put a robe on and go into this room where everybody scatters because of the radiation. You're lying alone on this table and the radiation is coming in and you're thinking, 'Well, they're giving me cancer while they're looking for cancer.' You just feel really creepy. Mother was a radiation technologist—I always thought maybe they didn't make her wear lead aprons. Anyway, I turned thirty and didn't die, so I felt really good about that."

MADONNA ON DEPRESSION:

"My treatment for feeling bad was not to make myself feel better but to flagellate myself in other ways."

MADONNA ON DILDOS:

"I've never had one inside of me, but for a joke I asked a friend of mine to put one on. I just couldn't stop laughing, so I don't see how anyone could look at them with a straight face."

MADONNA ON DOING DRUGS:

"I went through a real short period where I very begrudgingly tried a few drugs. . . . What I like[d] about it was that it took my edge off. I'm a naturally suspicious person, and all of a sudden I didn't see everyone as my enemy. I was really nice to people. . . .

"It was enjoyable a couple of times. But I would feel violently ill after I did it. I'd be bedridden for days, so it wasn't worth it. . . . I never really enjoyed coke because it made me more of a nervous wreck than I am."

MADONNA ON EARLY ASPIRATIONS:

"I would say, 'I'm going to be a nun,' like you would say, 'I'm going to be famous.' Then the nuns announced to me that a girl who wanted to be a nun was very modest and not interested in boys. After that, my role model was my ballet teacher, who was fabulous and demonstrative and extravagant. I wanted to be like him.

"I sometimes think I was born to live up to my name. How could I be anything else but what I am, having been named Madonna? I would either have ended up a nun or this."

MADONNA ON THE "F" WORD:

[Madonna once used the word *fuck* two hundred times in five minutes on British radio. Why did she do it?] "That was because it was *all* they wrote about [me]. . . . I decided that I was just going to say it all the time to make a point. . . . That's me being mischievous, sticking my tongue out at people and fucking with them for not having the *brilliance* to understand it in the first place. They don't get the humor. They take everything I do so seriously."

MADONNA ON FELLATIO:

"I'm a good kisser. I *know* that. . . . Everybody says so. They don't tell me I give good head, believe me, because I don't give it. . . . They just tell me I'm a savage bitch. Who wants to choke? That's the bottom line. I contend that that's part of the whole humiliation thing of men with women. Women cannot choke a guy. . . . It doesn't go down into their throats and move their epiglottis around."

MADONNA ON FINDING WORK:

"I ultimately end up making my own work. I don't sit around waiting for other people to give it to me. I've had to do this to ensure myself constant employment. I honestly don't think I could just announce to Hollywood. 'Okay, now I want to be an actress,' and then wait for people to give me movies. I also couldn't be just a recording artist who puts out a record once a year. I have to keep finding things for myself to do."

MADONNA ON GAY MEN:

"Well, people didn't talk about gay life in the Catholic Church. They barely talked about sex. So I didn't see it as something I was supposed to be wary of or afraid of. All I knew was I was attracted to Christopher [Flynn] and his lifestyle. I fell in love with him and the way he treated me. I started spending a lot of time with dancers, and almost every male dancer that I knew was gay. Then I went through another kind of feeling inadequate because I was constantly falling in love with gay men. Of course, I was so miserable that I wasn't a man."

MADONNA ON GETTING SLAPPED:

"My stepmother slapped me a lot, and she gave me a bloody nose once. . . . Trying to make ends meet . . . she would go to K Mart and buy big bolts of fabric that were on sale. She would sew the exact same McCall's dress pattern for me and my . . . sisters. I detested that—looking like my sisters. . . .

"We got into the car to go to church and I was disgusted that I had to wear this lime-green dress with white stripes on it. . . . I mumbled something about this horrible ugly dress I was wearing, and my stepmother just went BAM! I always got nosebleeds when I was little and my nose bled very easily. . . . I couldn't have been more thrilled. Not only did I not have to wear the dress, but I didn't have to go to church."

MADONNA ON GOD:

"I still believe in God. . . . I don't like to have to visit God in a specific area. I like Him to be everywhere. . . . Part of my air."

MADONNA ON HAPPINESS:

"Well, I'm a very tormented person, I suppose. I have a lot of demons I'm wrestling with. But I want to be happy. I have moments of happiness. I can't say I'm never happy. I'm working toward knowing myself and I'm assuming that will bring me happiness. I'm slowly getting rid of the demons. You see, I don't think you can truly be loved until you know and love yourself. Then, you can be truly loved and that's what I want."

MADONNA ON HAPPIEST MOMENTS:

"My most happiest moment recently was when I went home to visit my family for Christmas. And I was sitting on my father's lap and a lot of my brothers and sisters were there. And just hanging out and sitting on his lap and feeling like a little girl again. And knowing that I was making my father happy. That was my last happiest moment.

". . . My father absolutely does not acknowledge that I'm famous, or a star, or a celebrity, or that I've made it in any way. He doesn't talk about it, so I can fit in and not feel the scorn of my brothers and sisters. I'm not sure that I like that."

MADONNA ON HAVING CHILDREN AND WHEN:

"As soon as I find Mr. Right."

MADONNA ON THE IDEAL DATE:

"I'm dying to meet someone who knows more than me. I keep meeting guys who know less."

MADONNA ON LEARNING SHE WAS ATTRACTIVE:

"When did I think I was attractive? When I started hearing it from my ballet teacher at about sixteen. [Up to then] I thought I was a dog from hell."

MADONNA ON LESBIAN LOVE:

"Let's put it this way: I've certainly had fantasies of fucking women, but I'm not a lesbian. . . . After they give me head I want them to stick it inside of me."

MADONNA ON LOVING AND NOT LOVING:

"It's something of a cliché, but you can have all the success in the world, and if you don't have someone to love, it's certainly not as rewarding. The fulfillment you get from another human being—a child, in particular—will always dwarf people recognizing you on the street."

MADONNA ON MADONNA-PHOBIA:

"There's two different fears [men have of me]. There's the superficial fear they would have just because they'd read all these things about me. And if they've had the bad fortune to believe everything, then they would have a lot of preconceptions about me and probably be afraid and very guarded.

"Then there is the fear that they would have once they'd gotten to know me, which is that I am very much in charge of my life and a dominating and demanding person and a very independent person. A lot of men aren't ready to deal with that. . . .

"Everybody has their image that precedes them. My sexual image is looming out there in front of me. Everyone probably thinks that I'm a raving nymphomaniac, that I have an *insatiable* sexual appetite, when the truth is I'd rather read a book."

MADONNA ON MARRIAGE:

"You don't make those kinds of mistakes twice. . . . [This time] it'll be a side-dish kind of thing. . . . I wouldn't want to treat it like coleslaw or anything. I guess I'd just like to think of it as spa cuisine versus a full twelve-course meal."

MADONNA ON MEN'S OBSESSION WITH BREASTS:

"That's just a leftover thing with their moms."

MADONNA ON MISTER RIGHT:

"Smart. Confident. Smells good. Sense of humor. Likes to write letters. Likes antique jewelry. The three toppers are smart, smells good, confident. . . .

"Intelligence would be good. . . . I'll [even] take a slightly overweight guy if he's smart. . . . I'll put him through a training regime. But what can you do to somebody's brain? The die is cast. . . . I'm waiting for the perfect man."

MADONNA ON HER MOTHER'S DEATH:

"[When she died, I] said, 'Okay, I don't have a mother to love me; I'm going to make the world love me.' "

MADONNA ON A NORMAL HOME LIFE:

"There's something to be said for a domestic life and knowing somebody's there for you. I just think it's hard to live the life I lead and then have this happily married life. I haven't been successful at it so far, but who's to say I can't be? . . .

"I haven't met somebody who could take all of me, ultimately, who I think is my intellectual equal and truly understands me."

MADONNA ON PATIENCE:

"I'll never learn patience. But I've learned, watching Woody [Allen shooting a movie], how a real artist works. Woody is a master at getting things out of people in a really gentle way. He's not a tyrant, and that's good for me to learn because I can be something of a tyrant. In a working situation. Well, in a living situation, too."

MADONNA ON PENIS ENVY (MORE OR LESS):

[Madonna was asked if she would like to possess a penis.] "Yeah, I'd like to know what it feels like to go in and out of somebody. . . . It's enough having my breasts as an appendage. When you jump up and down, or dance, or run, or whatever, they're there. I can't imagine having a third thing hanging off my body. How dreadful! . . .

"[But] I'd really like to pee standing up. . . . That's what makes women vulnerable, that extra hole. . . . We have a big orifice that insects can crawl inside of. . . .

"I probably had that fear when I was little. Whenever I was out in the woods, I'd sit on my hands to make sure that no bugs could penetrate my underpants and go up inside my crotch."

MADONNA ON THE PERFECT GIFT TO GET:

"I've gotten some *really beautiful* jewelry from Warren [Beatty]. . . . He has excellent taste in jewelry: necklaces, rings, earrings, bracelets, pins, beautiful brooches—antique stuff. It's rare that a guy will give you really good jewelry. I was shocked, pleasantly. Most people just go out and use their own bad taste."

MADONNA ON PERSONAL RELATIONSHIPS:

"Yeah, I'm difficult on a lot of levels. Just my situation alone is pretty daunting and probably keeps a fair share of men away from me. You have to be prepared for your private life to be spilled to the world, because the minute you start going out with me, that's what happens.

"So they have to find that out and understand that their past is now public domain. I try to warn them, but you can never warn people completely. Some people take it very well and others are destroyed by it. It does affect my relationships."

MADONNA ON THE POWER OF PRAYER:

"I believe in everything. That's what Catholicism teaches you. . . . I don't [go to confession] now, but I did. . . . But mind you, when I did go to confession, I never told the priest what I thought I'd really done wrong. I'd make up other, smaller crimes. I thought, look, if I think I've done something wrong, I have a private line to God, and I'll just tell Him in my bedroom. . . . He knows my voice by now. . . . If something's really horrible and I say enough prayers, it will get better."

MADONNA ON POWER OVER PEOPLE:

"Power is attracted to power and power threatens power. And certainly people in a similar position to me understand better what I have to do. So I think that's probably a benefit. And anyway . . . I've fallen in love with people who aren't famous. The question is, can you maintain it? As long as the person has a sense of their own identity, that's what's important. What they do is irrelevant. . . . I give people a lot of room and . . . sometimes they're just begging me to come into the room."

MADONNA ON PRENUPTIAL AGREEMENTS:

"I'd have to be with somebody who I could ask for one. They'd have to be not insulted if I asked for one—bottom line."

MADONNA ON RELIGION:

"Catholicism is a really mean religion, and it's incredibly hypocritical. How could I be supportive of it as an organized religion? But it plays a role in my life, because you can't really get a lot of things out of your head, such as what Jesus Christ looks like and that divorce is a horrible thing."

MADONNA ON SAINTS:

"In terms of saints, when I was confirmed I took the name Veronica as my confirmation name because she wiped the face of Jesus. You know, you weren't supposed to help Christ while he was on his way to the Crucifixion; she was not afraid to step out and wipe the sweat off him and help him. So I liked her for doing that, and I took her name. There's Mary Magdalene—she was considered a fallen woman because she slept with men, but Jesus said it was okay. I think they probably got it on, Jesus and Mary Magdalene. Those are my saint heroes."

MADONNA ON THE SANDRA BERNHARD INCIDENT:

"Sandy and I have always been great friends. I think in the very beginning there was a flirtation, but I realized I could have a really good friend in Sandra, and I wanted to maintain the friendship.

"When I went on *The David Letterman Show*, it wasn't exactly clear how things were going to go. But Sandy started playing up that we were girlfriends, and I thought, 'Great, okay, let me go for it.'

"Because, you know, I *love* to fuck with people. Just as people have preconceived notions about gay men, they certainly do about gay women. So if I could be some sort of a detonator to that bomb, then I was willing to do that. It was really fun.

"Then, of course, it went highly out of control. Everybody picked up on it, and the question was 'Are we sleeping together?' It's not really important."

MADONNA ON SCHEDULING:

"I have to schedule everything. And that drives everyone I'm with insane. *Everyone.* They go, 'Can't you just wake up in the morning and not plan your day? Can't you just be spontaneous?' And I just can't. . . . I need to have an organized life. And I do. I probably pay a price for that, but this is what I wanted."

MADONNA ON SEAN PENN (I):

"I still love Sean and I understand very clearly, now that time has passed, why things didn't work out between us. I miss certain things about our relationship because I really do consider Sean to be my equal—that's why I married him. I don't suppose I've found that yet with anybody else."

MADONNA ON SEAN PENN (II):

"I have to see his movies because sometimes that's the only way I can see him. It's peculiar—especially with the last one, *State of Grace,* the one he did with his girlfriend—future mother of his child."

MADONNA ON SEAN PENN (III):

"We did make a really good couple . . . but we had our problems. I hate to keep talking about it. It's all over. But . . . there's something to be said about people being the love of your life. Even if it doesn't work there's always that person that you love.

"I did have a real connection with Sean and I still do. I feel close to him even though we're not physically close. Going through what we went through made us very close. There was a lot of pressure. I mean, it really is amazing we didn't kill each other. But I don't feel like it was a waste of time. I still love him."

MADONNA ON SEAN PENN (IV):

"I never slammed him publicly. But I went through a hostile period. My heart was really broken. You can be a bitch until your heart's broken, and then your heart's broken, you're a superbitch about everything except that. You guard that closely. . . .

"Then we went through a period where I never would have known I was even married to the guy. It was like that part of my life did not exist. Four years. The first year was good—sort of. [Getting married] was really a romantic thing. We were madly in love with each other, and we decided quite soon after we started seeing each other that we were going to get married—and then we got married."

MADONNA OF SELF-REGIMEN:

"I'm hardest on myself. If I have a seven o'clock call . . . I'll get up at four-thirty to exercise. If I don't, I'll never forgive myself. A lot of people say it's really sick and an obsession. Warren used to say I exercised to avoid depression. And he thought I should just go ahead and stop exercising and allow myself to be depressed. And I'd say, '*Warren*, I'll just be depressed about not exercising!' "

MADONNA ON SEX AND RELIGION:

"Your sexual life is supposed to be dead if you're a good Catholic. That's wrong. It's human nature to be sexual, so why would God want you to deny your human nature?"

MADONNA ON SEX EDUCATION:

"My stepmother told me [about sex], and I remember I was horrified. I was ten and had just started my period. It was like, 'Okay, we better tell her.' I remember my stepmother was in the kitchen, and I was washing dishes. Every time she said the word *penis*, I'd turn the water on really hard so it would drown out what she said. I thought what she was telling me was horrifying, absolutely horrifying. And I hated the word. I just hated the whole thing."

MADONNA ON SEX IN CHURCH:

"When I was a little girl, I was at church by myself on a Saturday afternoon going to confession because my father insisted. I don't know why now. No one was there, and instead of going out the main entrance, I went through this vestibule off to the side. . . . I opened the door a little bit, and there was this couple standing up fucking in the church. I thought, *Oh, my God!* I shut the door really fast. That's the only sex I've seen in a church. Seems like a neat thing to do, though."

MADONNA ON SEX TOYS:

"I'm not really interested in dildos. . . . I like the human body. I like flesh. I like things that are living and breathing. And a finger will do just fine. I've never owned a vibrator, if that's what you want to know."

MADONNA ON SEXUAL ALLURE:

"Marlene Dietrich is still sexy. . . . She's gorgeous. She had a very masculine thing about her, but I think she maintained a sexual allure."

MADONNA ON SEXUAL KINKS:

"I don't like blow jobs. [I like] getting head."

MADONNA ON THE SIZE OF A PENIS:

[Does the size matter to you?] "No."

MADONNA ON SUCCESS:

"I wonder if there are people walking around who are happy with what they've accomplished? I don't know *anyone* who's happy."

MADONNA ON VACATIONS:

"I never take any time off if I can help it. I've taken three vacations in the last ten years. All of them lasted about a week, and they were all in some tropical place. My boyfriend or husband at the time would want to go, and I'd agree. Actually, I'd finally give in."

MADONNA ON WORKOUTS:

"My whole life is in a constant state of disarray, and the one thing that doesn't change is the workout. If I had nothing to do, I would stay in the gym forever. It's a great place to work out aggression, or, if you're feeling depressed about something, you get on the Lifecycle and you forget it. If you've failed in every way in your day, you've accomplished one thing—you've gotten through your workout and you're not a total piece of shit."

Index